TRICKS & GAMES
ON THE
POOL TABLE

By
FRED HERRMANN

DOVER PUBLICATIONS, INC.
NEW YORK

Published in Canada by General Publishing Company, Ltd., 30 Lesmill Road, Don Mills, Toronto, Ontario.

Published in the United Kingdom by Constable and Company, Ltd., 10 Orange Street, London WC 2.

This Dover edition, first published in 1967, is an unabridged and unaltered republication of the work originally published by the "Tricks" Publishing Company in 1902 under the title *Fun on the Pool Table*.

Standard Book Number: 486- 21814-7
Library of Congress Catalog Card Number: 67-17985

Manufactured in the United States of America
Dover Publications, Inc.
180 Varick Street
New York, N. Y. 10014

PREFACE.

Doubtless a good many of our readers have seen tricks performed on the pool and billiard table by professionals and have considered them wonderful, which they most certainly are, and have been acquired only by a great deal of practice and patience; but how many amateurs would think of attempting to perform them? They know that they are beyond their power, so they are content, as a rule, to *speak* about them, and to *tell* their friends what they *saw*, but unfortunately they cannot *show* them how they were done. In this book we propose to show and illustrate with illustrations that there are many simple and amusing games and tricks on the pool table well within the reach of the most moderate pool player, shots that require no great execution or power of cue to perform, and yet are of sufficient difficulty and contain enough elements of fun to interest good and indifferent players alike, with *no risk of cutting the cloth.*

We have collected here some odd tricks and games, some of them old. This book may, however, be of use to you to refresh your memory, but to those to whom they are new it may serve to while away and afford amusement for an evening and help to relieve the tedium of a rainy hour or two.

CONTENTS.

CONTENTS

9

TO HIT THE TOP BALL FIRST.

Place two balls up against the top cushion, both balls touching, and balance another ball on top of them. (The way to balance the top ball is to rub some chalk in the palm of your hand and rub the ball on it, then it will adhere slightly to the other two balls.) Then play with another ball from balk. The trick is to hit the top ball first. For example: aim carefully at the top ball, hit your ball just sufficiently hard to reach the top cushion, and while the ball is travelling either thump hard on the table with the hand, or give the table a good push with the side of the body. This will cause the top ball to lose its balance, and it will roll gently and straight on to the table between the other two balls before your ball has had time to reach it, the other two balls getting out of the way, and your ball if struck accurately will hit it.

11

No. 2.

TO POCKET THREE BALLS IN ONE SHOT.

Place the red ball on the pyramid spot with a white ball absolutely touching it in a dead straight line with the left-hand corner of the left top pocket, as in illustration. The trick is to play with another ball from balk, and pocket all three balls in one shot. For example: Place the ball you are going to play with about two inches on the inside of the right-hand spot of the D. Aim to go in off the white into the left-hand corner top pocket, the other white should go into the right-hand top corner, and if you have placed the balls accurately and aimed truly, the red ball should follow yours into the pocket. Medium strength.

No. 3.

ROUND THE WOODWORK.

A very amusing game, and one that requires great steadiness of hand, is to take a ball right round the woodwork of a pool table with the side of a cue.

For example: Put a ball on the woodwork of the table, and put your cue on it about eighteen inches from the tip. Push it little by little without touching the ball with the hand; of course the difficulty lies in rounding the narrow rims of the pockets. It helps you to grip the ball if you chalk the sides of the cue.

Two can play this game at once by starting at different ends of the table.

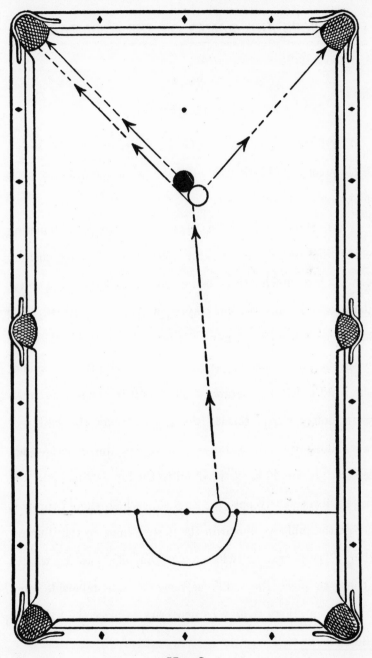

No. 2.

No. 4.

HAND CAROM.

The following carom can be done pretty regularly with a little practice, and though effective is not so difficult as it looks.

Place three balls as in illustration, two balls touching each other on one cushion, the other ball touching cushion exactly opposite, all three being in a straight line; the object is to make a hand carom, playing with a solitary ball. For example: Place the palm of the right hand against the ball with the fingers toward the bottom pocket, and the side of the hand touching the table. Then pull the right arm backward, fairly sharp, toward the top cushion—the ball will work along from the palm to the tips of the fingers—then let go. It should then travel on to the top cushion, and you have unconsciously put on "English," which should throw it across the table as shown in the dotted lines in the illustration. Try it once or twice to get the idea, and the whereabouts to place the balls; as some cushions take side more freely than others, it may be necessary to place the balls farther from or nearer to the bottom cushion.

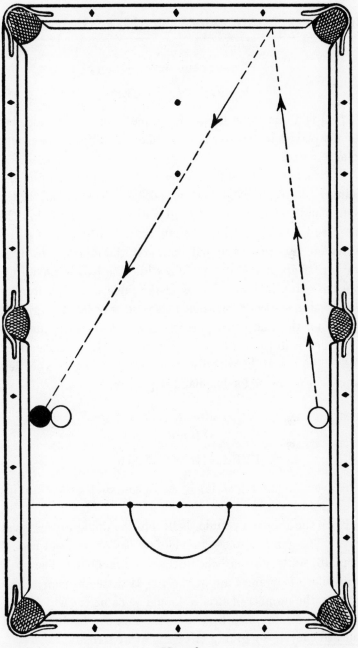

No. 4.

No. 5.

WEIGHT REDUCER.

This is a fine game for getting rapidly into condition, but is best played in the winter. It takes a really active person to accomplish it.

Place a cue on the table, close to the bottom cushion, tip pointing to right-hand bottom pocket. Take a ball in the right hand. The game is to roll a ball up the table, hit the top cushion with sufficient strength that when the ball returns and hits the cue it will jump off the table. See illustration for about the angle. But while the ball is travelling, you have to run round the top of the table and catch it, after it has jumped the table, but before it touches the ground. Stand for the start with the right foot level with the balk line, then roll the ball, and off you go. If you are quick you ought just to be round in time to catch it with your left hand. *Vice versâ* for left-handed players.

No. 6.

PYRAMID SOLITAIRE.

A good game for practice by one's self, and makes an interesting competition.

Place the fifteen pyramid balls on the table in the usual way. The game is to see in how few strokes you can pocket them all, starting from balk in the usual manner. The ordinary rules of pyramid are to apply. If there are many competitors, the number of strokes should be named at which each player must relinquish his attempt. You can handicap good and bad players by giving or taking away strokes.

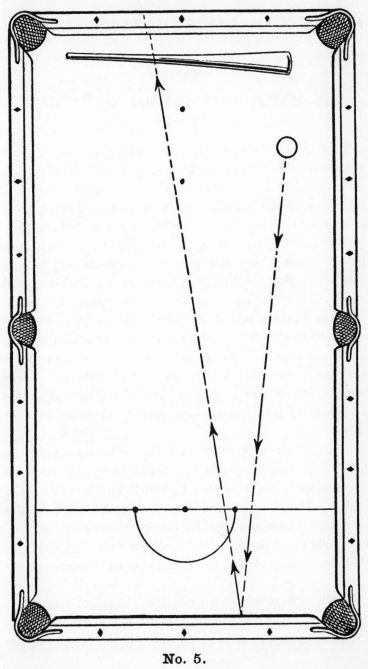

No. 5.

No. 7.

THE MATCH THAT CANNOT BE KNOCKED DOWN.

This is a very curious trick, and will give rise to much amusement, as it is apparently so easy to do. First, stand a match on the table—this may be done by slitting the end a little way up and spreading out, so as to form a small tripod arrangement, or by cutting a slit in a piece of card and placing the end of the match inside the slit; the card will then lie flat on the table. But both these methods must be on a very small scale, as the object is simply to make the match stand upright. Now place three balls round the match, each one touching the other. The match is then standing up in the small space left between the centre of the balls, but is not touched by any one of them. You then invite any one to try and knock the match down by placing their ball about two feet away from the three. They are at liberty to try from any direction outside the two-feet radius.

Strange to say, however hard the balls are struck, the match still remains upright; the reason being that, owing to the position of the balls, they kiss each other away from the centre. The shot, however, may be done by using a little thought. Those who try it for the first time think that they have only to hit the balls hard, and it is sure to go over; but the harder they strike, the firmer the match seems to remain.

One way is to make your ball jump on top of the others; but this is very difficult to judge, and I should not advise any but professionals to attempt it, owing to the danger of cutting the cloth.   The other way is to put your ball opposite one of the corners of the triangle and play a run-through shot.   Strike your ball well above the centre fairly hard; when it comes in contact with the first ball, it will rebound from the other two, but your ball following on behind will push it forward again, and the match will go over.

No. 8.

THE TRAVELLING BILLIARD BALLS.

This experiment can be accomplished with a fair amount of practice.   One cue is laid upon the table and a ball stood upon it; upon this first ball the second one is placed, and then the other cue is rested on top of both balls.   In this condition, by picking up both cues, the balls will remain

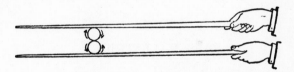

stationary, as in illustration.   By gently altering the position of the cues, both balls can be made to run backward and forward without overbalancing.   This is because one ball revolves forward and the other revolves in the opposite direction, as is explained by the little arrow upon either side of the balls.

This genuine experiment has been cleverly burlesqued by causing both balls to be attached to the topmost cue.   The underneath one is then removed, and the trick, as it were, shown up; this generally occasions a hearty laugh.

No. 9.

TO KNOCK A COIN FROM THE TOP OF A BALL OUT OF A SMALL RING.

Draw a small ring with chalk around the billiard spot three and one-half inches in diameter. Then place a ball on the spot and balance a coin on top of it. The trick is to hit the ball with another ball played from balk, and knock the coin away so that it falls outside the chalk ring. There are two ways of doing this, though neither of them is a certainty every time. The first way and the more difficult is to play with just sufficient strength to reach the object ball and to touch it so slightly that it turns very slowly over and throws off the coin. The other way is to aim so truly that your ball follows straight on after hitting the other ball, catches the coin and knocks it away before it has time to reach the table.

No. 10.

PASS BALL TRICK.

Place a red ball almost in the jaws of a pocket, and a white ball touching the cushion above it about a foot away. The trick is to pocket the white in the nearest pocket, playing with a cue, without touching the red, jumping over it, playing across the table, or a *massé* shot. For example: Take a cue and press the tip against the white, well below the centre, at the angle shown in illustration. This will cause the ball to run up on to the cushion, the cue remaining on top of the ball. Gently rotate the cue to the right, the ball will naturally travel to the left along the cushion past the red, and drop into the pocket.

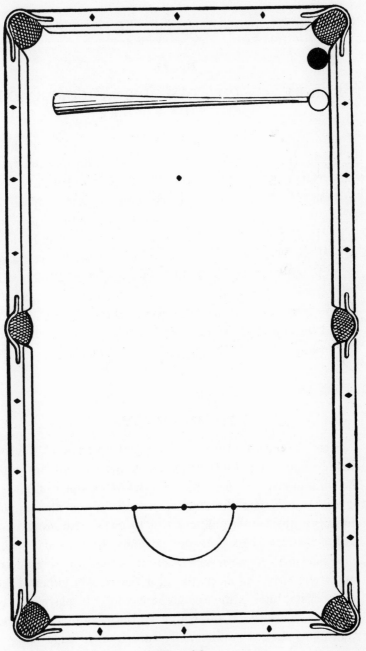

No. 10.

No. 11.

TO MAKE A COIN DESCRIBE A CURVE AND ROLL INTO A POCKET.

A quarter is placed on its edge resting against a cushion about two to three inches above the balk line, left-hand side, and a ball is laid at about the middle of the left-hand top cushion, which it touches. It therefore appears impossible to get the coin in the top left-hand pocket as the ball is apparently in the way, but with a little practice it may be done as follows: The coin, which is to be as nearly upright as possible, must be struck rather high on its edge or it will not roll, and if played properly it will describe a graceful curve right round the ball into the pocket. If the coin is placed leaning slightly and struck gently, it will roll along the cushion and drop into the middle pocket.

No. 12.

TRICKY CAROM.

Place the red ball tight up against the middle of the top cushion with a white ball touching it in a straight line with the billiard spot. Place the other white on the centre spot of the D, therefore the three balls should be in a straight line as in illustration. The shot is to make a carom playing with a ball from balk. It can be done from the side cushions, but it is by no means a certainty that way. To do it pretty regularly you must aim into the jaws of either of the top pockets, hitting the top cushion first. If played fairly hard, the ball will be thrown off by the jaws of the pocket right along the top cushion and your carom is made.

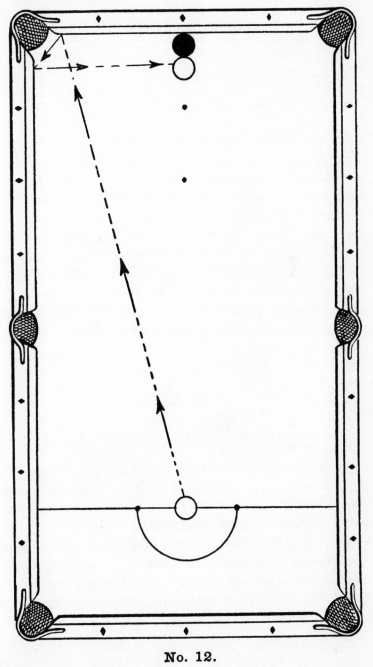

No. 12.

No. 13.

PYRAMIDS: ONE POCKET AGAINST FIVE.

This is an amusing game, and with equal players the odds are also equal. The game is: one player is to have only one pocket, usually the left-hand top corner; the other five belong to his opponent. Each player counts only the balls that go into his own pocket or pockets, no matter who puts them in. The player who takes the one pocket has the privilege of starting, his object being to get a ball over his pocket. The scheme for the player who takes the five pock-ets is to get all the balls down the table as quickly as possible. The one-pocket player should never try to take a ball hard unless he is certain of it, but should leave it over the pocket if it does not go in.

No. 14.

RUN A BALL OFF TWO CUES.

Place two cues on the table with the tips underneath a cushion and place a ball on them, as in illustration. The trick is to make the ball roll off the cues at the butts without letting the ball touch the table.

For example: Open the cues very gently and slightly until the ball commences to roll toward you. Get up as much speed as you can on the ball, then close the cues. If you do this at the right second, the ball will have sufficient way on it to roll up and over the ends. If not, it will run back again to the cushion.

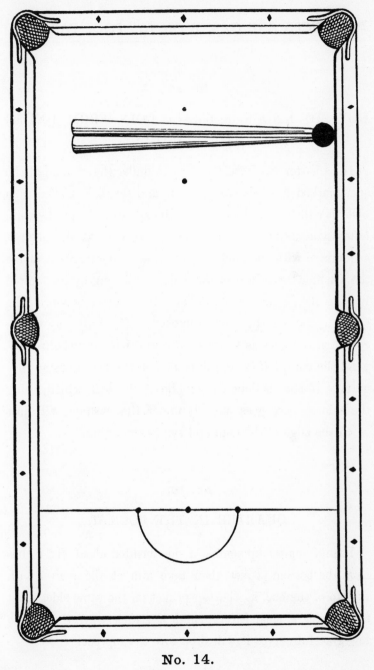

No. 14.

No. 15.

HOW TO KNOCK A SMALL COIN FROM UNDER THE CUSHION.

If a quarter is placed on its edge under the cushion at the spot marked A in the illustration, and the ball played from balk, it will be found extremely difficult to dislodge the coin, unless you are aware of the secret. If you ask any one not acquainted with the trick to do it, he will invariably strike the cushion exactly over the coin, as shown by the dotted lines in the diagram, but the ball will always rebound off the cushion, leaving the coin unmoved. The only way to accomplish the trick is to strike the cushion very slightly beyond the coin, following the course of the firm lines in diagram. If this is done the middle of the ball, which, being the widest part, goes slightly under the cushion, will just catch the edge of the coin and send it spinning.

No. 16.

QUARTER IN THE POCKET.

Lean a quarter up against a side cushion about six inches from the bottom pocket, then take aim at the quarter with the tip of the cue, at the top pocket on the same side. Hit the quarter a smartish tap, and if struck correctly, after a few graceful curves it will drop into the top pocket.

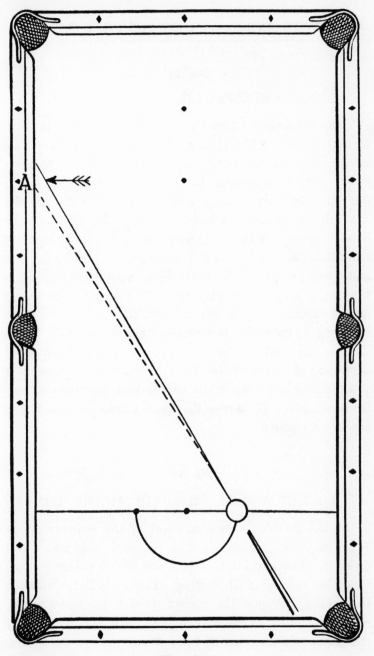

No. 15.

No. 17.

STEEPLE-CHASE SHOT.

There are several games on the billiard and pool table in which the knowledge of how to make one ball jump over another is extremely useful, but the fear of cutting the cloth deters many from making the attempt. It can be done in the following manner, and the cloth cannot be cut. Lay the cue full length on the table, then take the butt into the hand, holding it in the usual way, but so that the butt is not more than three inches away from the table. Place the first and second finger of the other hand over the cue near the tip, as though you were playing a ball through your fingers on the cushion. On no account raise the tip from the cloth, but drag it backward and forward along the cloth, in addressing the ball in the usual way. Hit moderately hard, depending of course on the distance you want to jump. If you hit your ball truly in the middle you can jump it perfectly straight. Of course this shot cannot be done if you are near a cushion.

No. 18.

TO POCKET A BALL THROUGH MATCH BOXES.

Get two outside covers of any sort of the ordinary match boxes, large size. Place them on the pool table with a ball on each. Put a third ball in a line with a pocket and the two other balls as in illustration. Play a hard shot with the ball on the table into the pocket through the match boxes, which should fly off the table, and the two balls will occupy the places where the match boxes stood.

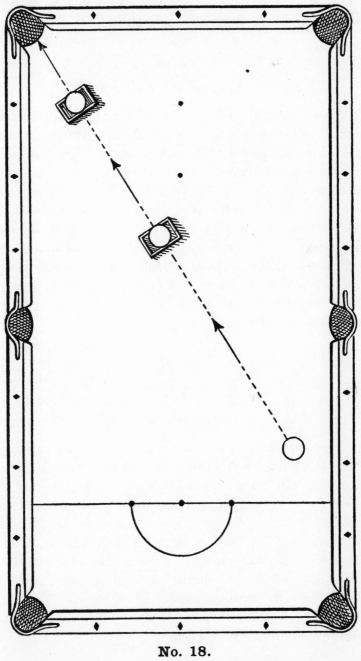

No. 18.

No. 19.

DECEPTIVE POCKET SHOT.

Place three balls in the middle of the table as in illustration. The trick is to play with a ball farthest from the red, and to pocket the red in the middle pocket. This is a trick in which the quickness of the hand has to deceive the eye. For example: Take up your position as though you were going to hit the ball in the usual way, but in reality don't look at the white ball at all. Keep your eye fixed on the red. Then with a very quick shot, push through the white ball, which will slightly separate and allow the tip of your cue to go through and hit the red and drive it into the pocket. If done very quickly it cannot be perceived. Try it slowly first to get the idea.

No. 20.

PASS THROUGH.

HAND SHOT.

Jamb two balls into a corner pocket perfectly squarely, and place a third ball tight up against the middle of them, touching both balls. The shot is to hit the ball farthest from the pocket and make it pass through the middle of the two other balls into the pocket. For example: Make a straight, sweeping shot with the palm of the hand at the top of the outside ball, straight at the middle of the pocket. If hit correctly the two inside balls will run away carrying the ball you hit with them about a foot, but the "English" you have put on your ball with the blow will cause it to run back again into the pocket.

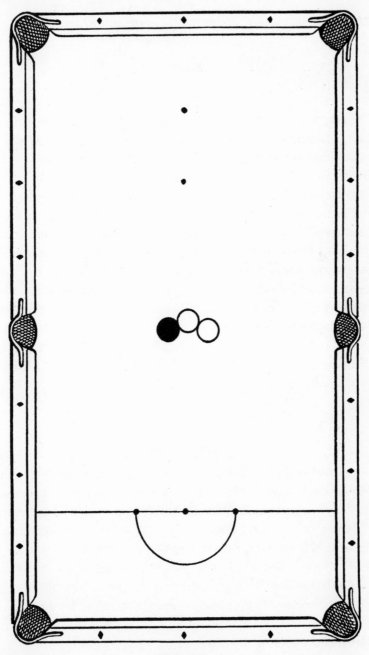

No. 19.

A PRETTY CAROM.

Arrange two cues, with the butt ends in the jaw of the top left-hand pocket, and place a ball on the top of them so that they will be jammed firmly in the pocket; they will then form a V with the thick ends touching. The ball on the top will then be fixed, and cannot be knocked into the pocket or run down cues. Now place the red ball midway between the open ends. To make the shot, play from balk, and, striking your ball rather high, hit the first cue about eighteen inches from its tip; the ball will then jump over the cue, and though not having enough strength to jump the second cue, it will be found that the ball has just sufficient impetus to reach the white ball at the butt end of the cues. After touching this, it will start to run down the incline, and, leaving the cues, it will run straight on to the red, getting the carom.

No. 22.

SQUEEZE SHOT.

A useful shot to know, playing the old rules, but is barred by the new ones. Place the red ball, touching a cushion, about fourteen to eighteen inches from a corner pocket and place a white ball, almost touching it, as in illustration. The shot is to pocket the red in the nearest pocket.

For example: Push the white up against the red and squeeze them against the cushion; hang on to it until both balls commence to run toward the pocket, then let go. The red should kiss in off the white into the pocket, although it frequently goes in straight.

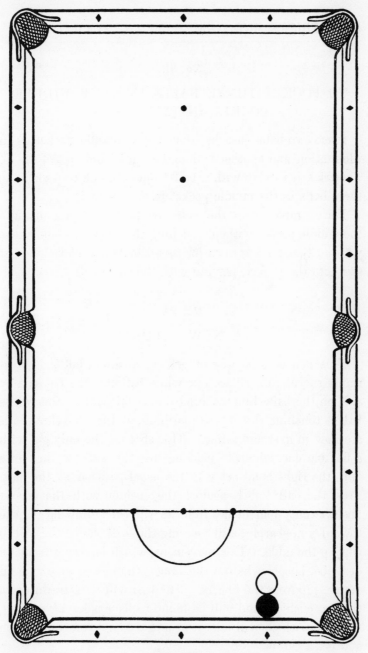

No. 22.

No. 23.

TO POCKET THREE BALLS IN SAME MIDDLE POCKET IN TWO SHOTS.

Place two balls just in front of the middle pocket as in illustration, and another ball on the right hand spot of the D. The trick is to play with a ball from balk and to pocket the three balls in the middle pocket in two shots.

For example: Aim the ball you play with straight into the middle pocket without touching the other two—of course you must just leave room for this—and then play the other two into the pocket, playing with the outer ball.

No. 24.

A NEW STROKE.

This is a peculiar way of getting a carom, but it is invariably successful. Place one white ball and the red side by side on the balk line touching the cushion, the other white ball is touching the opposite cushion, so that the three balls are now in a straight line. This shot can be only got with a flexible cue, which is held against the side of the white ball, the right hand being in the usual position at the butt. Press the ball tightly against the cushion with the cue, at about twenty-four inches from its tip, then drawing the cue toward you sharply, still pressing the ball, cause the ball to run up the table. This movement, which is very difficult to describe, is somewhat on the same principle as squeezing an orange pip from the fingers. The ball will then travel up to the top cushion, and will be found to have a lot of running side on it which will take it at a sharp angle off the cushion and get a carom.

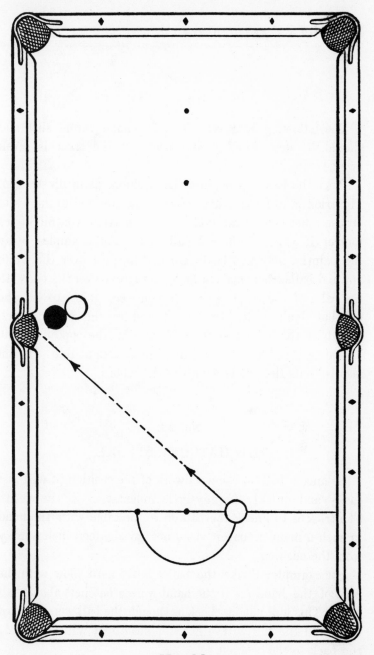

No. 23.

No. 25.

TRICK HAND CAROM.

The following is a very deceptive hand carom shot and should be done quickly and neatly or the trick is given away.

Place the balls up against the cushions as in illustration. The trick is to make a hand carom from the red to the white on the other side of the table. It is a trick you might try forever if you hit the red ball first. For example: Sway the palm of the hand backward and forward over the white and red balls, then make a sweeping stroke over the red with the palm of the hand as though you were going to hit the red, but don't do it, just miss it, and hit the white, which will drive the red across the table and hit the opposite white —that is, if you have put all three in a straight line. It can also be done the whole length of the table.

No. 26.

THE HATCHET STROKE.

Balance a ball on the woodwork of the cushion (it will rest easily and quickly in any little indentation in the wood). The trick is to knock the ball on to the table with the hand in such a manner that it does not go eighteen inches away from the cushion.

For example: Strike the ball a fairly hard blow with the edge of the hand (as if the hand were a hatchet) about half ball. This will put on check as though the ball were screwed back, and the ball will either stop dead or it will frequently run back to the cushion.

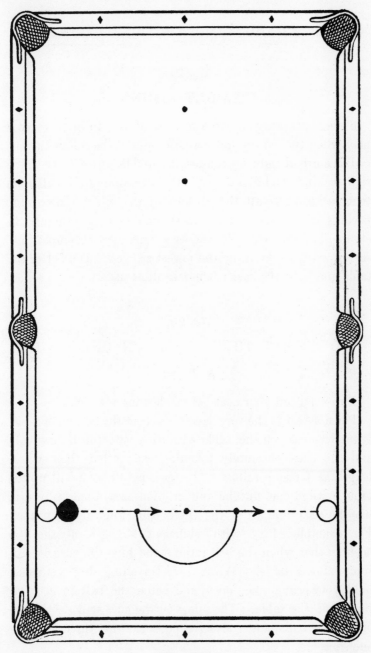

No. 25.

No. 27.

STRAIGHT AIMING.

To see whether you can aim straight and to improve your play when tucked up under a cushion, try the following:

Place a ball tight up against the middle of the top cushion right behind the billiard spot. Practise aiming the ball from that position into all the pockets of the table; the two top pockets are of course easy, but the middle and bottom pockets require practice. It makes a fairly good competition, seeing who can do it in the fewest strokes. The better the table and balls the easier it is (see illustration).

No. 28.

TO POCKET THREE BALLS IN ONE SHOT.

A Trick.

Please put on your coat before showing this trick.

Place a ball in the very jaws of each of the bottom pockets. Place two cues on the table with each butt touching a ball, and the cues absolutely touching each other their whole length as far as possible. The trick is to play a ball up the table with a cue, hit the top cushion first, then to return, hit the cues and all of the three balls to go into a pocket. For example: Play with sufficient strength at the top cushion that when the ball returns and hits the cues it will jump off the table. While it is travelling drop your cue, hold your coat pocket open, and catch the ball in it as it jumps off the table. The blow on the cues will pocket the other two balls, and you have pocketed the three balls in one shot.

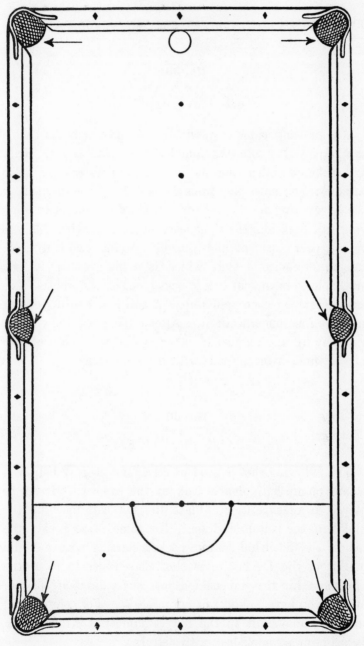

No. 27.

No. 29.

POOL DECK QUOITS.

An amusing game of quoits on the pool or billiard table can be played as follows: Complete the circle D with chalk and make two other rings as shown in the illustration. The game is: You must play from the balk line on either side of the largest ring and hit the top cushion first, and try to bring your ball back into the rings, each of them having different values, your opponent and yourself playing two balls each, tossing for choice of start, which is a disadvantage, as you are liable to have your ball knocked out of the rings. The usual game is eleven points up. A ball is not in if you can see the line underneath it. After hitting the top cushion you may hit any number of other cushions. It can also be played three or more a side with the same rules.

No. 30.

BALK PRACTICE.

The following shot is good practice, and it may help you when you are left a double balk, at the same time it can be played as a competition. Place the red ball touching the middle of the bottom cushion. The game is to pocket the red in the left-hand bottom pocket, starting with a white ball from the D; but every shot played has to be up the table and hit the top cushion first, never direct at the red, even if you have to knock it out of balk. For competition, the one who does it in the fewest number of strokes wins. It has been accomplished in two strokes.

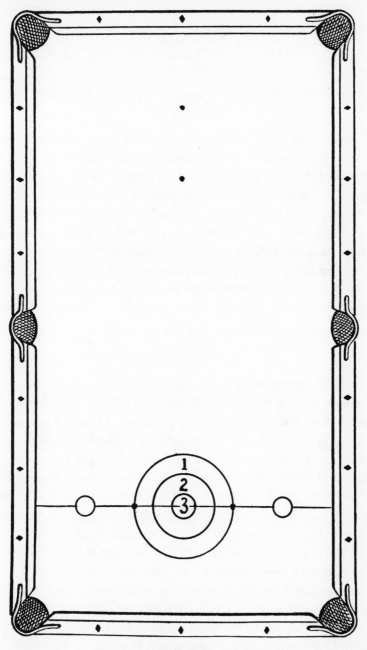

No. 29.

No. 31.

TO POCKET THREE BALLS IN TOP POCKET IN ONE SHOT.

Put a ball into the jaws of each of the top pockets and a third ball on the middle spot of the D. The trick is to pocket the three balls in one shot, playing with the ball in balk. For example: Put two cues on the table as in illustration, but not until after your victim has failed to accomplish the shot. Hit the outside cue with a little left-hand side on your ball, as per dotted lines; the left cue pockets one ball and you are bound to run down the right cue. Hit the ball and follow it into the pocket; not too hard.

No. 32.

CAROMS *VS.* PYRAMIDS.

This is an amusing game, especially with a good hazard-striker, against whom a moderate player ought not to make more than about forty to fifty caroms. Place the pyramid balls on the table in the usual way; one player has to see how many caroms he can make before the other pockets the pyramid balls. For example: The hazard-player plays first from balk, and has a smash at the pyramid. If a ball goes in he continues playing until he fails. Then the carom-player begins. He plays with the white at any two balls he likes; but if his ball is touching another one, or if a ball goes into a pocket whilst he is making his caroms, or if he fails to carom, he has to give way to the pocket player, who goes on until he fails, and so on alternately, until only one pyramid ball is left. With a good hazard-striker not so many caroms are made as one would imagine.

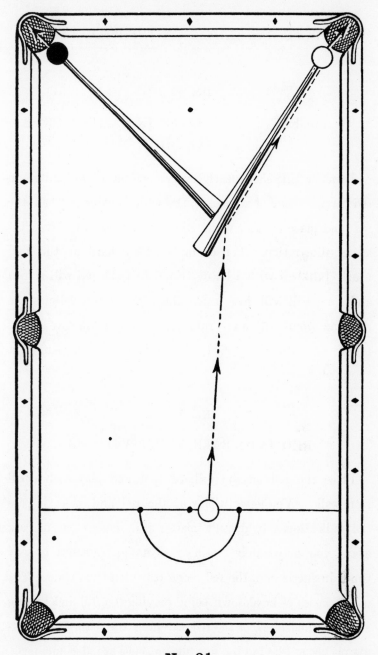

No. 31.

No. 33.

TO POCKET THREE BALLS IN SAME POCKET IN ONE SHOT.

To make this shot nearly every time place the white and red in the jaws of a pocket, the white nearer in than the red, and place another white (the one you are to play with) as in illustration. For example: Play hard at the red, nearly full ball with a lot of "English"; the red will run in and your ball will just touch the white which follows the red, and your ball after running back a little way should follow on into the pocket, if you have put on sufficient "English."

No. 34.

RED INTO BALK TWENTY TIMES.

Place the red on the billiard spot, and play with a ball from balk. You have to play at the red and make it pass the balk line. It doesn't matter if it comes out of balk again, you may safely bet against its performance twenty times in succession, the red being respotted each time. The usual causes of breakdown being playing too full and kissing off the top cushion, or the red catching the bump of a middle pocket. Playing too fine and miscues are also enemies.

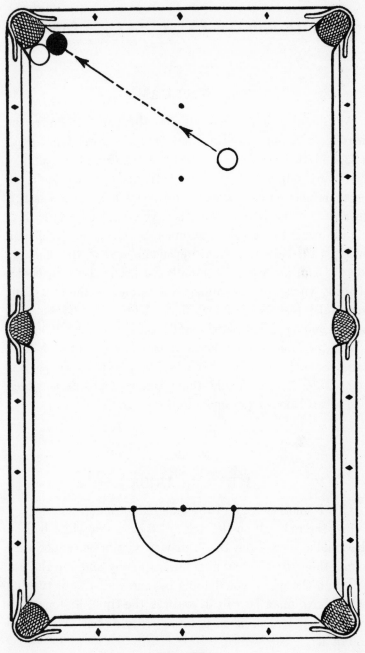

No. 33.

No. 35.

THE WAR GAME.

Any number of players can play this game, the more the merrier; it is quite exciting and provokes great fun. Skill tells, and there is a great element of chance. For example: Place any number of balls on both ends of the table, an equal number on each side, as in illustration. If the skill is greater on one side than the other, you can handicap by giving the weak side a ball or two more. The game consists in bringing the balls from your opponents' end of the table, up to your end, *i.e.*, past the middle pockets. Toss for choice of start, which is an advantage, the winner of the toss electing to let his side play first shot. Then the other side has a shot, and so on alternately until the balls are all on one side of the table or the other. A ball in a pocket is a dead ball. Should a ball be exactly half-way between the pockets you toss for it, and should there be any doubt as to which side a ball belongs you must do the same.

No. 36.

WET CUE TRICK.

This is another trick of the grandfather order.

Put the red ball on the billiard spot and a white ball on the middle spot of the D. Tell your victim he cannot turn round three times, then aim fairly quickly and hit the red ball with the white, you holding his cue whilst he is turning round. No more he will if you wet the tip of his cue with your tongue whilst he is gyrating, only do not let him see you do it.

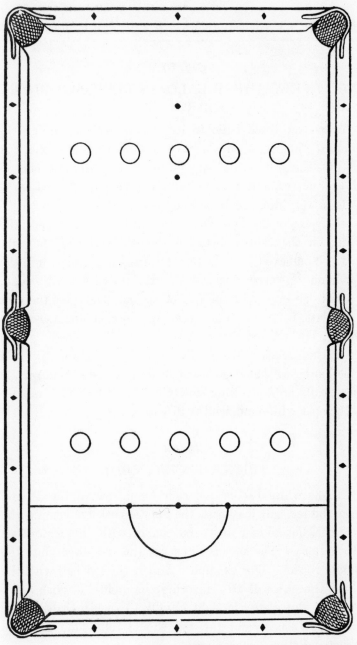

No. 35.

No. 37.

TO POCKET THREE BALLS IN REVERSE ORDER.
TOP POCKET.

To pocket three balls in the bottom pocket, sending one round the angles, is baby's play compared to this one. It requires the greatest delicacy of touch and absolute control of the nerves, and without a true table and a good set of balls is very difficult to accomplish. Place the three balls on the spots of the D. The red on the left corner spot, the white on the centre spot, and the spot white on the right spot. You have to hit the red ball first; it has to go into the left-hand top corner pocket last. Hit the white ball second, it has to go into the same pocket second; and play the spot white last, it has to go into the same pocket first. For example: Hit the red ball with only just sufficient strength to reach the pocket. Move quickly to the white and hit it a trifle harder so that it gets just in front of the red, and while these balls are travelling slowly up the table move rapidly to the spot white and send it in with a bang.

No. 38.

TRICKY POCKET SHOT.

Place a white ball on the right-hand spot of the D, and place the red ball just past the middle pocket, touching the cushions, but too far up to be cut in with the white (see illustration). The shot is to pocket the red direct into the middle pocket. For example: Aim at the red ball with the white almost a full ball, favoring the right "English" just a little. Put plenty of right "English" on your ball, and if you hit it just right the red should roll round into the pocket. Rather a slow shot.

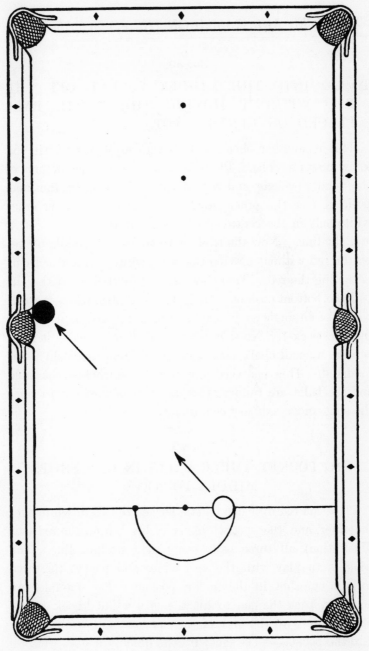

No. 38.

No. 39.

TO GO INTO THE MIDDLE POCKET OFF THE RED WITHOUT MOVING THE WHITE BALL PLACED ON CENTRE SPOT.

This is another shot which is very mystifying until you know how its done.   Place the red on the edge of one of the middle pockets, and one of the white balls in the same position over the other middle pocket; then put the other white ball on the centre spot so that all the balls are in a straight line.   Now the trick is to go in the middle pocket off the red without moving the other white ball and without pocketing the red.   This may be done by striking with your ball the bottom cushion exactly in the centre, when the ball will take an angle so just as to touch the red, and will go into the pocket.   No side is required, and to make it more certain, a small chalk mark can be made on the cushion beforehand.   This is a very good test to see whether the table and the balls are running true, as it is impossible to miss the shot under ordinary conditions.

No. 40.

TO POCKET THREE BALLS IN ONE SHOT, MIDDLE POCKETS.

Place the red over one middle pocket, the plain white over the other, and the spot white six inches behind the red (see illustration), all three balls being in a straight line.   The trick is to play with the spot white and pocket the three balls in one shot in the middle pockets.   For example: As you draw back the cue to hit the spot white knock in the plain white with the butt of the cue, and follow on the red into the pocket—a six shot; if done quickly it goes well.

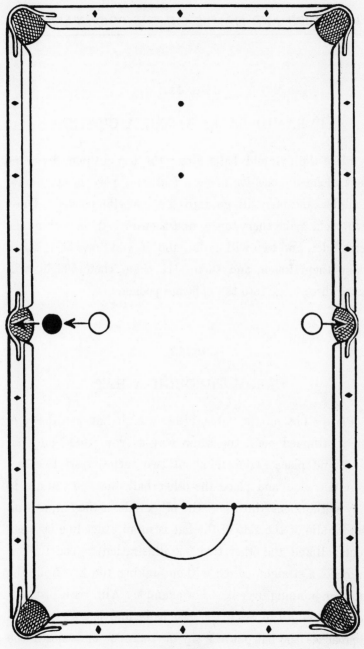

No. 40.

No. 41.

PYRAMID BALLS ALONG A CUSHION.

Place the pyramid balls along the top cushion, draw one back along the cushion about a foot, and play it at the remainder, and one will go into the opposite pocket. Draw two back, make them touch, and then play them both at the remainder, and two will go in, and if you draw back three, make them touch, and then play them, their weight will cause three to go into the opposite pocket.

No. 42.

CAROM THROUGH A HAT.

Place a hat on the table, either a high hat or a derby (a curly brimmed one), the same way as you would on your head, and place two balls about two inches apart two feet from one side, and place the other ball, the one you are to play with, about three feet the other side of the hat, so that the middle of the side of the hat is in an exact line between your ball and the other two (see illustration). The trick is to make a straight carom without taking the hat from the table or jumping over it. For example: Aim with just sufficient strength to reach the two balls, and just as your ball approaches the hat put the tip of your cue underneath the

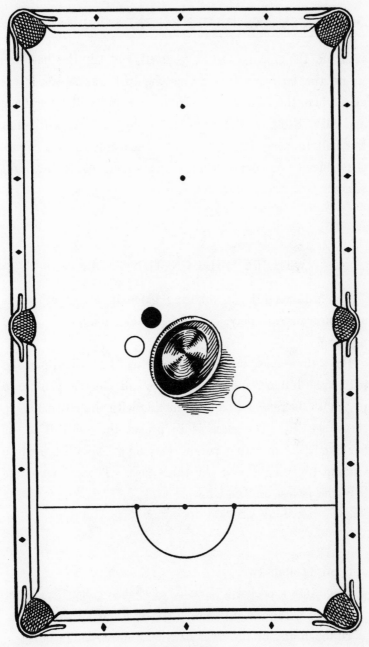

No. 42.

brim on the side nearest to yourself, and tilt the hat well up on the farther brim, just as the ball gets to about the spot where the brim rested let go. The hat will come down and raise itself on the brim nearest to you, and will allow the ball to pass out on the other side and make a carom, the difficulty of course being to let go the hat at the right second.

No. 43.

THREE CUES ON THE TABLE.

The following is an amusing game for a competition as any number can play. It doesn't take long, and is good practice.

Place three cues on the table, as in illustration, put the red on the billiard spot, and a white ball, the one you are to play with, behind it in a straight line with the left-hand top corner pocket. The game is to pocket the red ball in the left-hand bottom corner pocket, playing at it with the white without touching any of the three cues. The one who does it in the fewest strokes wins.

RULES.

A miss counts two.

To go into a pocket a burst—*i.e.*, chance gone.

To pocket the red in a wrong pocket a burst.

To touch any of the three cues with either ball a burst.

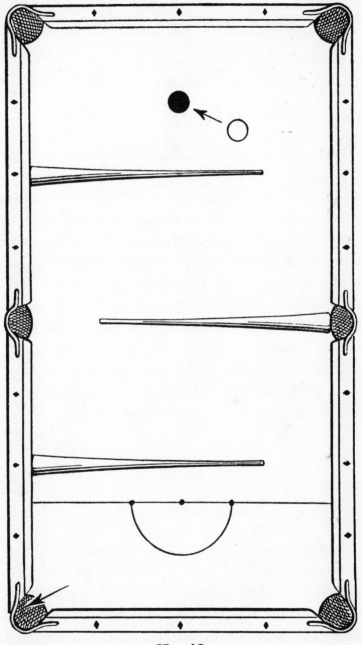

No. 43.

No. 44.

HAND POCKETING COMPETITION.

This is another hard-working game played by two players.

The game is to roll a ball by hand into every pocket of the table, two players starting at once, one at the left-hand bottom pocket, the other at the right-hand top corner, so that the two balls have to pass each other. Wait for the word "Go!" and then both start together, care being taken not to scratch the cloth with the nails, nor should the balls be played hard. If your ball goes in you recover it yourself, and go facing the next pocket. If the ball does not go in, you must recover it yourself and try again from the old position. The pockets have to be done in order, moving round to the left till you have done them all. Whichever finishes first wins. (See diagram for order of pockets.)

No. 45.

THE RUNNING SHOT.

An amusing game and one that requires judgment of pace.

Place a ball anywhere in the D of balk and get some one to roll a play or ball across the pyramid spot from side cushion to side cushion at a moderate to a hard pace, varying it every time. The game is to hit the ball whilst it is travelling,

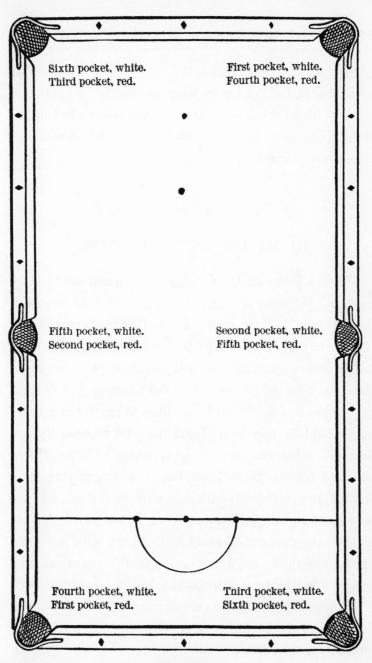

No. 44.

playing with the ball from balk.   As the ball is not always hit or rolled, the same pace judgment has to be used as to when to hit your ball so as to strike the moving ball up the table.   The shot should be made as the ball comes back from the first cushion.

No. 46.

TO HIT THE LAST BALL FIRST.

This is a pretty trick, requiring firmness and steadiness of hand and judgment of pace; the number of balls used will depend entirely on the agility and skill of the performer.

Place any number of balls in a straight line, about three to four inches apart, and the ball you are to play with about three feet from the nearest ball.   For the purpose of illustration I have put eight balls in the illustration, though a larger number of balls may be used and the trick successfully performed.   What you have to do is to play with the solitary ball and hit the farthermost ball, the red, playing in a straight line, without touching an intermediate one, and yet only removing one ball at a time out of the way.   For example: Aim at the farthermost ball, the red, with just sufficient strength to reach it, then, with the cue about two inches from the tip and while the ball is travelling knock a ball away with a sweeping stroke right and left alternately, leaving only the last ball.   The more strength you use the quicker you have to be.

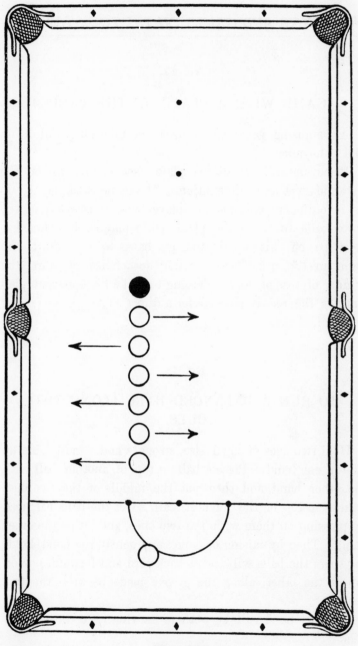

No. 46.

No. 47.

GAME WITH A PLATE ON THE TABLE.

An amusing game which does not take long, full of fun and annoyances.

Place an ordinary dinner plate, face downward, on the pyramid spot as in illustration. The game is to play 15 up as in ordinary pool, but the player who causes any of the three balls to touch the plate while playing his shot, has to wipe off his score and go back to 0. Start the game in the usual way, tossing for choice of start, the winner of toss of course electing to make his opponent play first, as the red is covered for a direct shot. Misses count as usual.

No. 48.

TO RUN A BALANCED BALL ALONG TWO CUES.

Hold two cues of equal size, strongly and steadily side by side in one hand. Place a ball on top of another ball with the other hand, and then put the middle of the two cues lightly on top of the topmost ball. Get the balls balanced by pressing on them with the two cues, and let go the other hand. Then by raising or depressing gently the hand holding them the balls will travel backward and forward, one on top of the other, along the groove made between the two cues.

A steady hand will keep them moving for a considerable time.

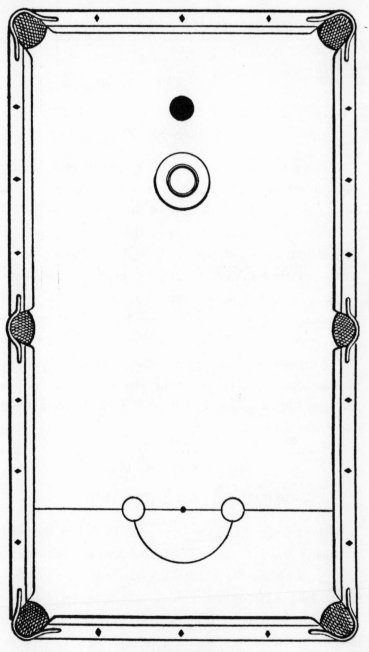

No. 47.

No. 49.

TO POCKET THREE BALLS IN THREE POCKETS IN ONE SHOT.

This is a very effective shot, but great care must be exercised in accurately placing the balls.   Place the white a little in front of the middle spot of the D, with the red ball touching it, in a direct line with the outside bump of the left middle pocket, *i.e.*, about three inches above centre of pocket.   Place a third ball a little in front of the right-hand bottom pocket as in illustration.   The shot is to play with the solitary ball at the other two and send a ball into each of the pockets on the left-hand side.

For example: Go in off the white slowly into the left-hand top corner pocket; the white should kiss off into the left-hand bottom pocket, and the red from the blow should travel into the middle.

No. 50.

SOLITAIRE, OR TABLE GOLF.

Without doubt this is the finest game to play by one's self. It teaches strength, angles, position, caution, and winning hazards; is amusing and makes a good round game, not taking too long.   Place the red on the spot in the middle of the table.   The game is to pocket it in every pocket of the table in order, commencing with the left-hand top corner pocket

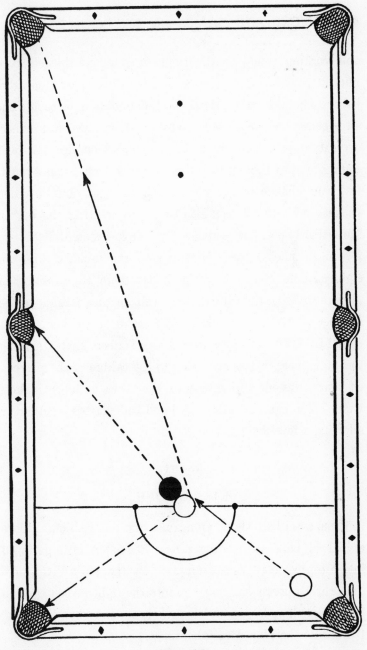

No. 49.

and working round to the right, finishing at the left-hand middle pocket. You play with a white ball, starting from balk. The red is replaced on the middle spot each time after being pocketed, but the white ball is played from wherever it stops. The rules for a competition are: A miss counts two; if the white ball goes into a pocket it is a burst, *i.e.,* your chance is over; if the red ball goes into a wrong pocket—a burst. It can also be played spotting the red on the billiard spot, but is about three strokes more difficult; or it can be played three times round the table, making an eighteen-hole course as in golf. If there are a number of players waiting their turn, it is well to put a limit to the number of strokes each player may make before being compelled to retire. If once around, say sixteen shots; making the limit more or less according to the calibre of the players. Of course the one who does it in the fewest number of shots wins. You can also bring good and bad players together by allowing a few shots.

No. 51.

KISS IN OFF.

Place a red ball tight up against the top cushion. Place a ball in balk as in illustration. The shot is to go in off into a top pocket. For example: Hit the red a little more than three-quarter ball. To go into the right pocket, put on left "English"; to go into left pocket, put on right "English." It need not be played very hard.

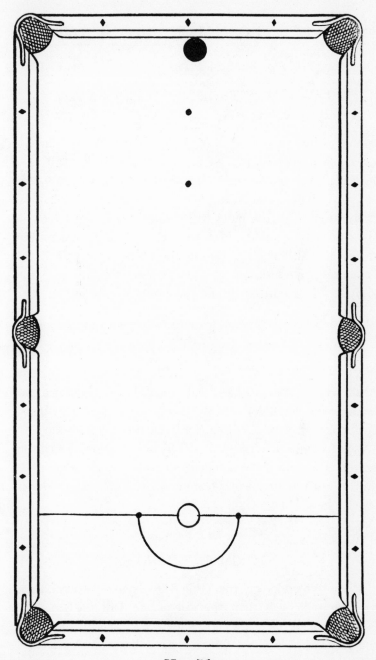

No. 51.

TO CAROM WITHOUT TOUCHING A BALL.

To carom without touching a ball or blowing it along of course seems an impossibility, but when you know how to do it, it is very simple. Place a red and white ball close together, and another ball close to them in position for the simplest of all possible caroms (see illustration). The trick is to carom with the outer ball without touching or blowing the ball. Impossible. Not so. For example: Take a pin, raise the cloth slightly behind the white outer ball, it will roll and make a carom and you haven't touched it. How simple. This will not injure the cloth.

No. 53.

THE LUNG TEST.

To try whether you have really good lungs, place two cues together on the table, with their butts resting up against a cushion, and place a ball on the two cues, down by the tips. If you have good lungs, you will be able to blow the ball up on the cues, and make it touch the cushion. It is easier to do this with a succession of short, jerky puffs, rather than a steady, hard blow.

No. 54.

CAROM TWO CORKS.

Place two corks on the table, the distance between them to be a trifle less than the size of the ball. Place a ball fairly opposite the space between the corks, and try to carom the two corks—a direct carom. Very disappointing.

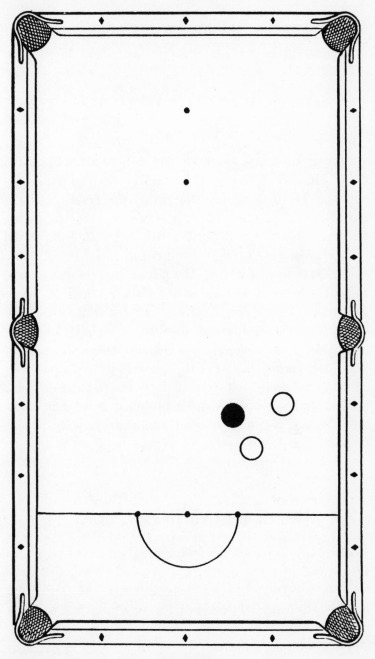

No. 52.

No. 55.

TO POCKET THREE BALLS IN REVERSE ORDER.

BOTTOM POCKET.

This trick requires quickness and self-control. Place the three balls one on each spot of the D, as in illustration, the white on the left-hand spot, the red on the middle, and the spot white on the right-hand spot. The trick is to pocket all three balls in the left-hand corner pocket in balk, in the reverse order of hitting. You have to hit the spot white first, and it has to go into the pocket last, the red second, and it has to go in second, and the plain last, and it has to go in first. For example: Send the spot white round the angles (see line in illustration), then move quickly to the right side of the table, hit the red just sufficiently hard to reach the pocket, then hit the plain white and send it in quickly, passing the red. By the time the plain white is in, followed by the red, the spot white should have gone round the table, and if you have found your angle correctly, should drop into the pocket last.

No. 56.

CAROM LENGTH OF THE TABLE.

Place two balls absolutely touching each other tight up against the top cushion. Play with a ball about a foot away from the bottom cushion and make a carom. If you do not hit the balls accurately between the two, your ball will kiss off, which happens quite as frequently (with moderate players) as the carom is made.

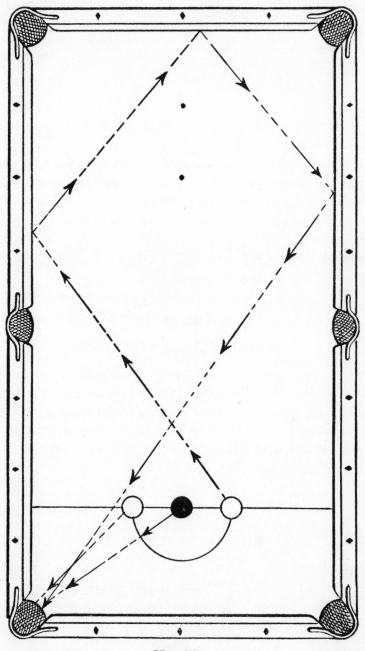

No. 55.

No. 57.

CAROM INTO A HAT.

Place a red ball against the top cushion and a white ball about eighteen inches a little to one side of it, and a hat with a white ball in it about eighteen inches to the other side of it, as in illustration. Play with the white ball at the red, hitting it a little to the right of the centre. Hit down at the ball you play with a fairly hard shot, and as soon as your ball hits the red it should jump into the hat. In hitting down at the white the butt of the cue should be about level with the top of the shoulder.

No. 58.

STEADY HANDS WANTED.

Place an ordinary square of billiard chalk on the table about a foot from one of the side cushions. Take a cue in each hand and from the opposite side of the table try to lift up the chalk with the tips of the cues and place it on the cushion. It is easy if you hold both cues with both hands; if only one hand touches each cue it is very difficult.

No. 59.

STOP SPINNING BALL

Rather an amusing trick is to get some one with strong fingers who can spin a ball well to spin one on the table and then you try to stop it dead by placing one finger on top of it. If it is spinning hard it is difficult. It cannot be stopped by placing the side of a cue on it. Try.

No. 57.

No. 60.

KNOCK DOWN A MATCH.

Make a match stand up upon the billiard spot, and place two balls, which must touch each other, in front of it, as in illustration.   The trick is to play from balk with another ball and knock down the match, of course without the aid of the cushion.   It is never very easy, but the way it comes off most frequently is to "follow" through one ball with a lot of "English": left "English" for the right-hand ball, right "English" for the left-hand ball.

No. 61.

TO PICK UP A QUARTER.

Place a quarter anywhere on the table.   The trick is to lift it off the table with the tip of the cue.   For example: Place the tip of the cue on the edge of the quarter nearest to yourself.   Press down gently but firmly, drawing the cue toward yourself.   The quarter should turn over on the cue and balance itself there, and you can lift it from the table.

No. 62.

TO BALANCE A COIN.

Stand a coin on its edge between two balls on the billiard spot, a steady hand will soon balance it.   Then play with another ball from balk at the two other balls, and try and knock down the coin.   You will find it stands up as frequently as you knock it down.

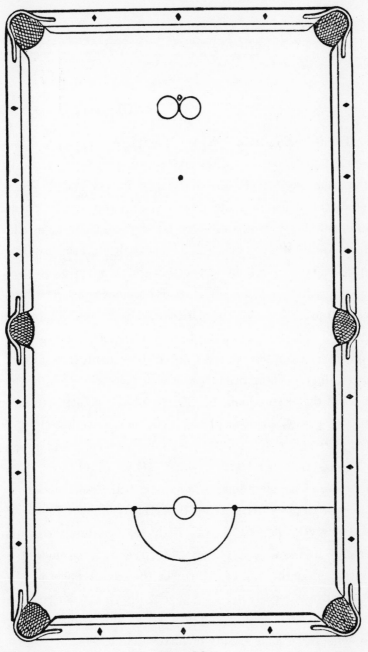

No. 60.

No. 63.

TO POCKET A WINEGLASS.

The following trick comes as a surprise to many, and as a rule long odds are bet against its performance, but in reality the odds are considerably in favor of its being done. Remove the balls from the table before beginning. Get an ordinary sherry glass and roll it gently on its side along the table to see that it has a little bias—that is, when rolling it describes part of a circle, one that rolls straight on is absolutely useless. The trick is, to lay it up against a cushion as in the illustration, and with a push to roll it into and make it disappear in the bottom pocket on the same side. When once you have found the spot to place it, it is almost a certainty. To find the correct spot, place the glass in the jaws of the bottom pocket with the mouth pointing toward the top pocket same side, then place a finger on the stem of the glass and give it a little push off. It should roll round on to the right-hand side cushion. Carefully observe where the base of the glass touches, and you will then have about the spot to place the glass for the return journey. It is well to know your glass to dispense with these preliminaries. Be careful in pushing if off not to let it slide along under the finger; place the pad of the tip of the second finger on the stem, give one push and let go. See illustration for position and the line the glass should go. Try it with several glasses, as some make more extensive curves than others.

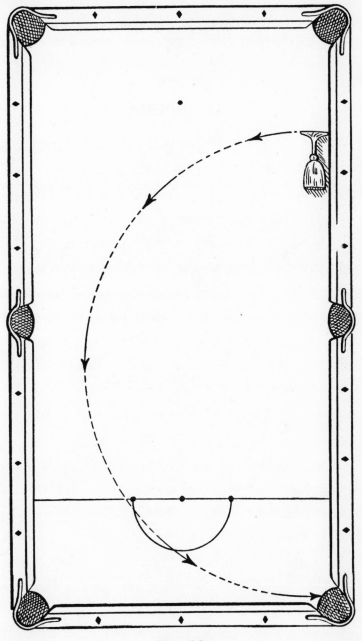

No. 63.

No. 64.

RACE HORSES.

An amusing and speculative game, although it cannot be played with much fun unless there is an amateur book-maker, who, as a rule, makes a nice little profit. Lay a cue on the table up against an end cushion, and put some pool balls up against it in any order as in illustration. The booky pushes the balls straight down the table with the cue, hard or soft according to the general desire, and removes the cue. That ball wins the race which is nearest to the cushion where they started from when they have all stopped. To facilitate the betting, draw some chalk lines along the cushion and number the spaces between them, one space for each ball running. These numbers refer to the pool balls in the usual order of play: No. 1 white, No. 2 red, No. 3 yellow, etc. Anybody wanting to back his color places the stake on its number. There should always be one ball running for the bookmaker, therefore he should lay odds as follows: However many balls are running he should lay one point less than their number to 1. Eight balls running, 7 to 1, etc. Dead heats of several sometimes happen, when the stakes are divided. When one race is squared up, start again.

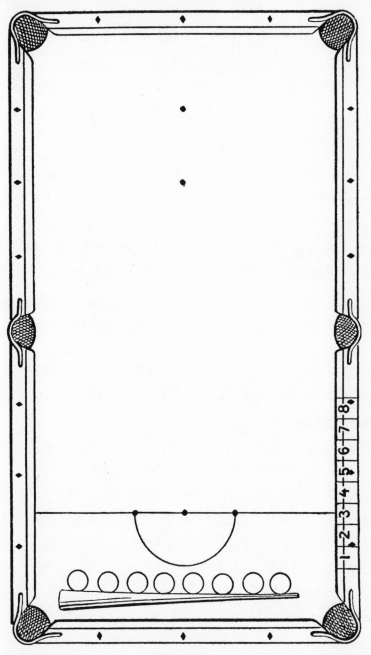

No. 64.

No. 65.

INTERESTING TRICKS IN ELASTICITY.

The clever trick with pool balls shown in Figs. 1 and 2 depends for its success on a truly scientific principle. A number of pool balls are placed in a row against the cushion of the table. The player asks one of the spectators to name a certain number of balls to be pocketed without any apparent disturbance of the others. Suppose the number to be three. Then at the will of the player three balls separate from the others and roll into the pocket. The number is perfectly controllable, and when the hand of the player and one end of the row of balls are covered, the trick appears mysterious. It is hardly less so when the entire experiment is visible. The feat is accomplished by removing from one end of the series as many balls as are to be projected from the opposite end, and rolling them forward against the end of the row remaining. An equal number of balls fly off from the opposite end of the row and roll into the pocket. Three balls driven against one end of the series will cause three to roll off, two will drive off two, one will drive off one, and so on.

The principle of this trick is illustrated in the well-known class-room experiment in which a series of contracting sus-

pended balls of highly elastic material are made to transmit
a blow delivered on the first of the series to the last ball of
the series, so that the last ball will fly off without any apparent disturbance of the other balls.   In this experiment,

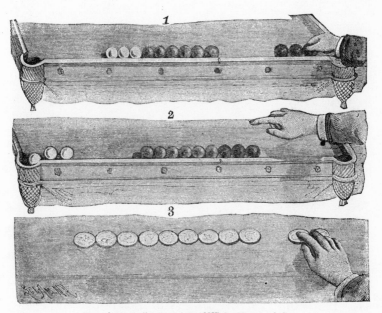

From " Magic."   Copyright, 1897, by Munroe & Co.

the first ball of the series is drawn back and allowed to fall
against the first one of those remaining in contact.   The impact of this ball will slightly flatten the ball with which it
comes in contact, and each ball in turn transmits its momen-
tum to the next, and so on through the entire series, the last
of the series being thrown out as indicated.

In the case of the experiment with the pool balls. it is found by careful observation that separate blows are given to the series, corresponding in number to the number of balls removed, so that while the separation of the balls at the end of the series is apparently simultaneous, in reality they are separated one at a time.

In Fig. 3 is illustrated a method of repeating the experiment with coins in lieu of balls. Dollars or half-dollars may be used, and the effect is produced by sliding the coins.

No. 66.

TO POCKET THREE BALLS IN THE OPPOSITE MIDDLE POCKET IN TWO SHOTS.

Place the red and the white ball touching each other in the middle of the table, straight between the middle pockets, and place a third ball in balk, as in illustration. The trick is to pocket the three balls in the middle pockets in two shots, the two balls in the centre of the table to go into opposite middle pockets. For example: Play the ball in balk into one of the middle pockets, then hold your cue tightly by the butt with one hand and hit down sharply and truly between the two balls on the table, which should separate and each go into a middle pocket.

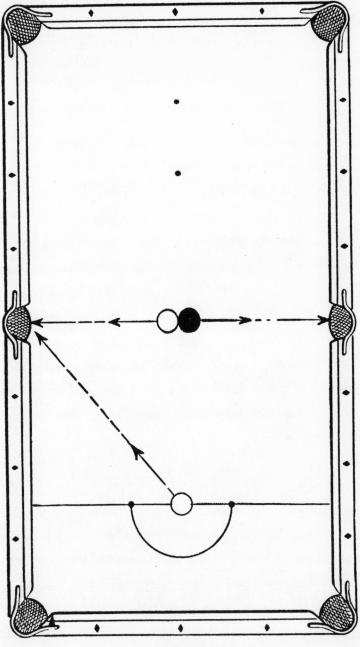

No. 66.

No. 67.

CHANCE ENCOUNTER CAROM.

The following is a pretty shot when it comes off, but is by no means a certainty. Place the red and white, touching each other against a cushion, the red ten inches from the pocket, the white inside it, and place another white four inches behind the white ball touching the red. The shot is to make a carom at the bottom of the table, playing with the ball nearest the pocket. For example: Hit the white about quarter ball right, with sufficient strength for your own ball to go over to the opposite cushion and then cross over to the bottom pocket. The red from the impact will travel straight and slowly down the table, and if you have just gauged the strength the two balls should meet. (See illustration for the idea.)

No. 68.

ONE BALL ON THREE.

Put three balls together and try to balance another ball on top of them. You will find this very difficult to do unless you chalk the top ball on the spots where it will rest on the other balls. To chalk it successfully, rub some chalk into the palm of the hand and rub the top ball on it.

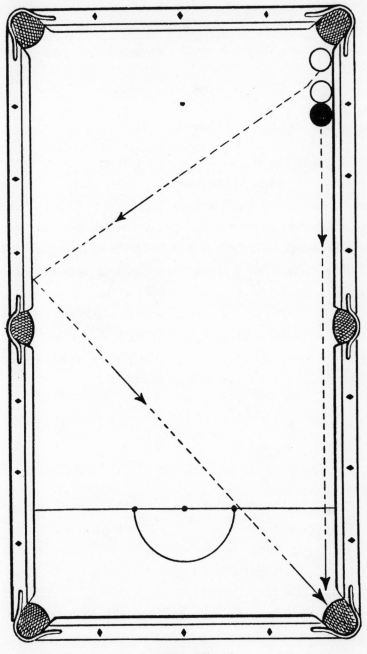

No. 67.

No. 69.

FINE CAROM.

A pretty carom can be made by placing the balls in the positions shown in illustration. Place the red twenty inches from the top pocket, touching the cushion, with a white touching it on the inside (*i.e.*, nearer the middle), and place another white ball in balk ten inches from the right-hand cushion. The shot is to play with the ball from balk and make a carom from the red to the white. For example: Although you can hardly see the red, it is fairly easy to hit it, of course very fine. Put right "English" on your ball, and you should come back on to the white after hitting the top cushion. See dotted lines in illustration.

No. 70.

PICK UP A BALL WITH TWO OTHERS.

Take a ball in each hand, and try and pick up another ball by squeezing it between the balls held in either hand. For example: Press the two balls in the hands, one on each side of the very centre of the third ball, as tightly and truly as you can. If you press accurately and sufficiently hard you can lift it from the table, if not it will slip out and run away on one side or the other.

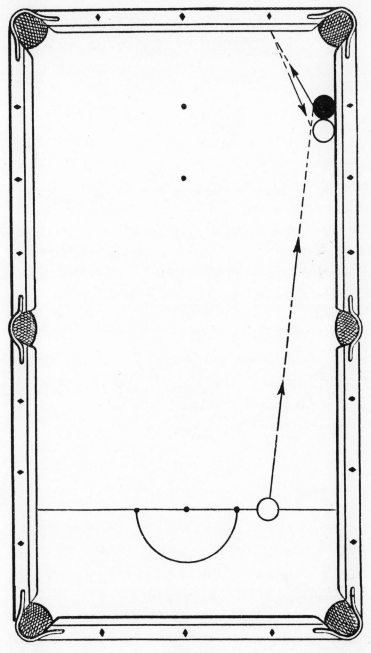

No. 69.

No. 71.

TO POCKET FOUR BALLS IN FOUR SHOTS.

Place five balls on the table as in illustration. The game is to pocket four of them in four shots in the top pockets, only playing with the ball from balk. The player must be satisfied to do it once in a good many attempts. It can be played as a competition, the one who does it in the fewest strokes winning. The idea is, play first at the ball on the right-hand cushion with the ball from balk, play it so that it proceeds slowly along into the right top corner pocket, getting position behind the ball on the spot. Play that one into the left-hand top corner pocket, and try to get down behind the ball on the pyramid spot; send that one into the right-hand top corner pocket, and cross over behind the remaining ball, sending it along the cushion into the left-hand top corner pocket. (See illustration for idea.)

No. 72.

COLLISION SHOT.

Stand close up against the top or bottom cushion, take a ball in each hand, strike them together, not too hard, as close to the middle of the cushion as you can hold them, and let go suddenly. If struck together properly, both balls touching the cushion at the time, they should disappear one in each of the end pockets.

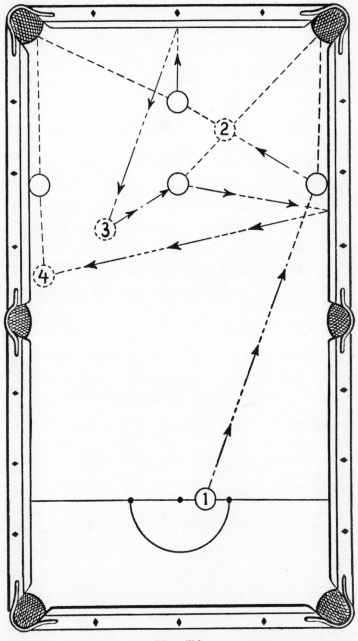

No. 71.

No. 73.

TO JUMP A COIN INTO A GLASS.

To make a coin jump from the cushion into a wineglass.

Place an ordinary wineglass on the woodwork of the table, and place a coin on the cushion at a distance varying from a quarter to three-quarters of an inch from the edge (depending greatly on the hardness or softness of the cushion, as in illustration). Place your ball about a foot from the opposite cushion, in a dead straight line with the coin and middle of the glass. Aim at the coin on the cushion, a moderately hard blow, and it should jump up and fall into the wineglass. One or two trial shots will soon show you how hard to hit your ball and the exact spot to place the coin on the cushion. It can also be done the whole length of the table.

No. 74.

ENDLESS CAROMS.

Put three balls side by side touching. Press the two outer ones *firmly* on the table. Withdraw the middle one, and hit it gently straight through the gap it originally occupied. It will make a double carom on passing between the other two balls, and if the stroke is played sufficiently gently, the two balls when hit will not be displaced from the

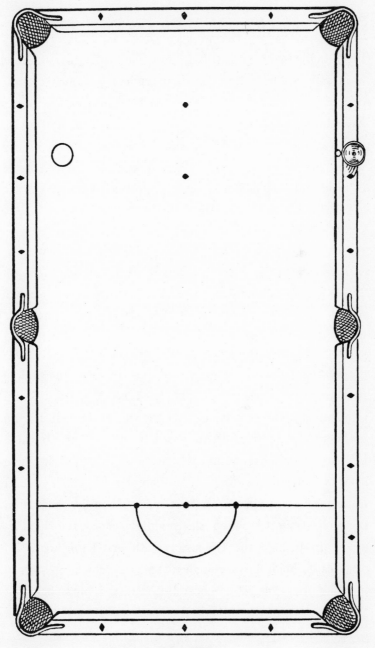

No. 73.

little hollows in which they rest, but will just oscillate, eventually settling down in their original position. A second double carom can now be made by hitting the object ball through the gap in the opposite direction, and so on backward and forward. A fair player with a good eye when once he has judged the correct strength, should be able to make quite fifty double caroms consecutively.

No. 75.

TO POCKET THREE BALLS IN THREE DIFFERENT POCKETS, THREE SHOTS.

Place a ball on the pyramid spot, and another on the middle spot of the D, and a third ball just in front the middle pocket, as in illustration. The trick is: You must stand tight up against the middle pocket where the ball is, and without moving from there you have to pocket all three balls in three shots, one in each pocket of the table the same side as you are standing. For example: Knock the one in nearest to you with the butt of cue. Then lay the cue on the table straight between the middle pockets, the tip toward yourself, hold the tip steady with one hand, with the other catch hold of the cue about half-way down, and sweep it along the cloth at a moderate pace, on to first one and then the other of the balls on the spots, and they should each go into an end pocket.

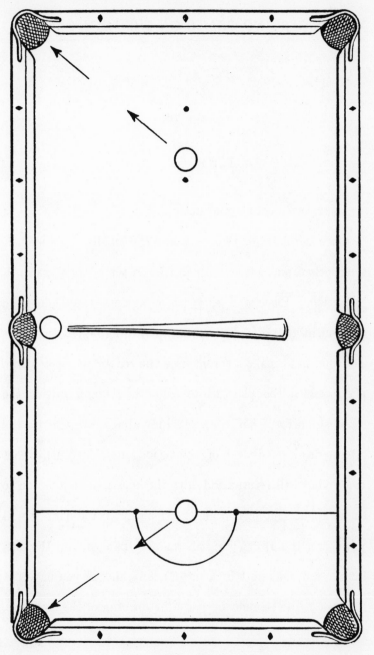

No. 75.

No. 76.

SWITCHBACK CAROM.

An effective carom, and not difficult.

Place the butts of two cues into the left-hand corner bottom pocket, and place the red ball on top of them, as in illustration. Place the spot white against the right-hand cushion in a straight line with the opening of the two cues. The shot is to make a carom from the red to the spot white, playing with the plain white from the D, and hitting the top cushion first. For example: Play almost straight up the table, with a good deal of right side, sufficiently hard that when your ball returns and hits the cues it will jump on to them about one foot from the tips (if hit too hard it will jump over them). Your ball should then run up the cue, hit the red, and start back down again, and if you have put the spot white straight opposite the opening of the two cues, it must hit it.

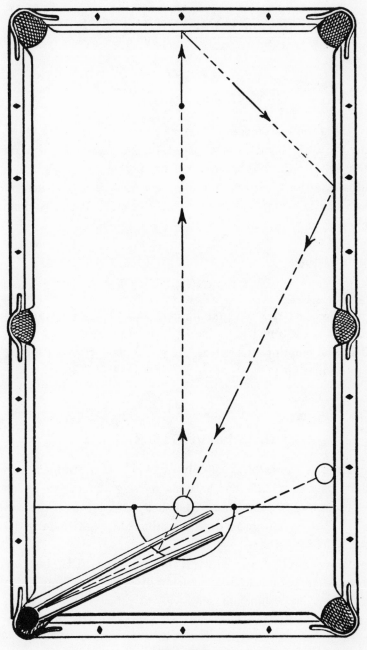

No. 76.

No. 77.

FINE OFF RED BALL.

Place the red on the middle spot of the table and a white on the right-hand spot of the D. The shot is to go in off the red into the left-hand corner top pocket (see dotted lines of illustration). It wants doing, but there is a good margin as you will see if you fail to hit the red. It can be done hard or soft.

No. 78.

WET FINGER TRICK.

This is a trick our grandfathers did. Place your middle finger on a ball and press hard till it slips away, and make it go the length of the table. If you do not wet your finger, you cannot do it.

No. 79.

THE IMPERCEPTIBLE JUMP.

Place three balls absolutely touching in a straight line; draw out the middle one without moving the others, about one foot away from them. The shot is to play with the cue at the ball drawn away from the others, through them without touching either.

For example: Aim straight between the balls, but hit down slightly at your ball, which will cause it to jump quite imperceptibly, sufficient, however, to allow it to pass between the other two without touching. Hit the ball pretty hard.

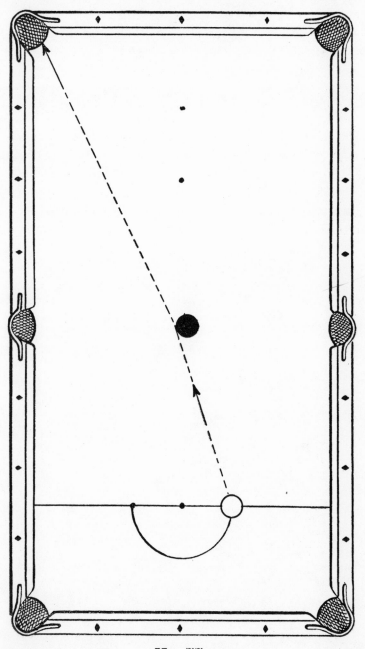

No. 77.

A CATALOGUE OF SELECTED DOVER BOOKS
IN ALL FIELDS OF INTEREST

A CATALOGUE OF SELECTED DOVER BOOKS
IN ALL FIELDS OF INTEREST

THE NOTEBOOKS OF LEONARDO DA VINCI, edited by J.P. Richter. Extracts from manuscripts reveal great genius; on painting, sculpture, anatomy, sciences, geography, etc. Both Italian and English. 186 ms. pages reproduced, plus 500 additional drawings, including studies for Last Supper, Sforza monument, etc. 860pp. 7⅞ x 10¾.   USO 22572-0, 22573-9 Pa., Two vol. set $15.90

ART NOUVEAU DESIGNS IN COLOR, Alphonse Mucha, Maurice Verneuil, Georges Auriol. Full-color reproduction of Combinaisons ornamentales (c. 1900) by Art Nouveau masters. Floral, animal, geometric, interlacings, swashes — borders, frames, spots — all incredibly beautiful. 60 plates, hundreds of designs. 9⅜ x 8¹/₁₆ .   22885-1 Pa. $4.00

GRAPHIC WORKS OF ODILON REDON. All great fantastic lithographs, etchings, engravings, drawings, 209 in all. Monsters, Huysmans, still life work, etc. Introduction by Alfred Werner. 209pp. 9⅛ x 12¼.   21996-8 Pa. $6.00

EXOTIC FLORAL PATTERNS IN COLOR, E.-A. Seguy. Incredibly beautiful full-color pochoir work by great French designer of 20's. Complete Bouquets et frondaisons, Suggestions pour étoffes. Richness must be seen to be believed. 40 plates containing 120 patterns. 80pp. 9⅜ x 12¼.   23041-4 Pa. $6.00

SELECTED ETCHINGS OF JAMES A. McN. WHISTLER, James A. McN. Whistler. 149 outstanding etchings by the great American artist, including selections from the Thames set and two Venice sets, the complete French set, and many individual prints. Introduction and explanatory note on each print by Maria Naylor. 157pp. 9⅜ x 12¼.   23194-1 Pa. $5.00

VISUAL ILLUSIONS: THEIR CAUSES, CHARACTERISTICS, AND APPLICATIONS, Matthew Luckiesh. Thorough description, discussion; shape and size, color, motion; natural illusion. Uses in art and industry. 100 illustrations. 252pp.
21530-X Pa. $3.00

TEN BOOKS ON ARCHITECTURE, Vitruvius. The most important book ever written on architecture. Early Roman aesthetics, technology, classical orders, site selection, all other aspects. Stands behind everything since. Morgan translation. 331pp.
20645-9 Pa. $3.75

THE CODEX NUTTALL, A PICTURE MANUSCRIPT FROM ANCIENT MEXICO, as first edited by Zelia Nuttall. Only inexpensive edition, in full color, of a pre-Columbian Mexican (Mixtec) book. 88 color plates show kings, gods, heroes, temples, sacrifices. New explanatory, historical introduction by Arthur G. Miller. 96pp. 11⅜ x 8½.   23168-2 Pa. $7.50

CREATIVE LITHOGRAPHY AND HOW TO DO IT, Grant Arnold. Lithography as art form: working directly on stone, transfer of drawings, lithotint, mezzotint, color printing; also metal plates. Detailed, thorough. 27 illustrations. 214pp.
21208-4 Pa. $3.50

DESIGN MOTIFS OF ANCIENT MEXICO, Jorge Enciso. Vigorous, powerful ceramic stamp impressions — Maya, Aztec, Toltec, Olmec. Serpents, gods, priests, dancers, etc. 153pp. 6⅛ x 9¼. 20084-1 Pa. $2.50

AMERICAN INDIAN DESIGN AND DECORATION, Leroy Appleton. Full text, plus more than 700 precise drawings of Inca, Maya, Aztec, Pueblo, Plains, NW Coast basketry, sculpture, painting, pottery, sand paintings, metal, etc. 4 plates in color. 279pp. 8⅜ x 11¼. 22704-9 Pa. $5.00

CHINESE LATTICE DESIGNS, Daniel S. Dye. Incredibly beautiful geometric designs: circles, voluted, simple dissections, etc. Inexhaustible source of ideas, motifs. 1239 illustrations. 469pp. 6⅛ x 9¼. 23096-1 Pa. $5.00

JAPANESE DESIGN MOTIFS, Matsuya Co. Mon, or heraldic designs. Over 4000 typical, beautiful designs: birds, animals, flowers, swords, fans, geometric; all beautifully stylized. 213pp. 11⅜ x 8¼. 22874-6 Pa. $5.00

PERSPECTIVE, Jan Vredeman de Vries. 73 perspective plates from 1604 edition; buildings, townscapes, stairways, fantastic scenes. Remarkable for beauty, surrealistic atmosphere; real eye-catchers. Introduction by Adolf Placzek. 74pp. 11⅜ x 8¼. 20186-4 Pa. $3.00

EARLY AMERICAN DESIGN MOTIFS, Suzanne E. Chapman. 497 motifs, designs, from painting on wood, ceramics, appliqué, glassware, samplers, metal work, etc. Florals, landscapes, birds and animals, geometrics, letters, etc. Inexhaustible. Enlarged edition. 138pp. 8⅜ x 11¼. 22985-8 Pa. $3.50
23084-8 Clothbd. $7.95

VICTORIAN STENCILS FOR DESIGN AND DECORATION, edited by E.V. Gillon, Jr. 113 wonderful ornate Victorian pieces from German sources; florals, geometrics; borders, corner pieces; bird motifs, etc. 64pp. 9⅜ x 12¼. 21995-X Pa. $3.00

ART NOUVEAU: AN ANTHOLOGY OF DESIGN AND ILLUSTRATION FROM THE STUDIO, edited by E.V. Gillon, Jr. Graphic arts: book jackets, posters, engravings, illustrations, decorations; Crane, Beardsley, Bradley and many others. Inexhaustible. 92pp. 8⅛ x 11. 22388-4 Pa. $2.50

ORIGINAL ART DECO DESIGNS, William Rowe. First-rate, highly imaginative modern Art Deco frames, borders, compositions, alphabets, florals, insectals, Wurlitzer-types, etc. Much finest modern Art Deco. 80 plates, 8 in color. 8⅜ x 11¼. 22567-4 Pa. $3.50

HANDBOOK OF DESIGNS AND DEVICES, Clarence P. Hornung. Over 1800 basic geometric designs based on circle, triangle, square, scroll, cross, etc. Largest such collection in existence. 261pp. 20125-2 Pa. $2.75

150 MASTERPIECES OF DRAWING, edited by Anthony Toney. 150 plates, early 15th century to end of 18th century; Rembrandt, Michelangelo, Dürer, Fragonard, Watteau, Wouwerman, many others. 150pp. 8⅜ x 11¼.   21032-4 Pa. $4.00

THE GOLDEN AGE OF THE POSTER, Hayward and Blanche Cirker. 70 extraordinary posters in full colors, from Maîtres de l'Affiche, Mucha, Lautrec, Bradley, Cheret, Beardsley, many others. 9⅜ x 12¼.   22753-7 Pa. **$5.95**

SIMPLICISSIMUS, selection, translations and text by Stanley Appelbaum. 180 satirical drawings, 16 in full color, from the famous German weekly magazine in the years 1896 to 1926. 24 artists included: Grosz, Kley, Pascin, Kubin, Kollwitz, plus Heine, Thöny, Bruno Paul, others. 172pp. 8½ x 12¼.   23098-8 Pa. $5.00
23099-6 Clothbd. $10.00

THE EARLY WORK OF AUBREY BEARDSLEY, Aubrey Beardsley. 157 plates, 2 in color: Manon Lescaut, Madame Bovary, Morte d'Arthur, Salome, other. Introduction by H. Marillier. 175pp. 8½ x 11.   21816-3 Pa. $4.00

THE LATER WORK OF AUBREY BEARDSLEY, Aubrey Beardsley. Exotic masterpieces of full maturity: Venus and Tannhäuser, Lysistrata, Rape of the Lock, Volpone, Savoy material, etc. 174 plates, 2 in color. 176pp. 8½ x 11.   21817-1 Pa. $4.50

DRAWINGS OF WILLIAM BLAKE, William Blake. 92 plates from Book of Job, Divine Comedy, Paradise Lost, visionary heads, mythological figures, Laocoön, etc. Selection, introduction, commentary by Sir Geoffrey Keynes. 178pp. 8½ x 11.
22303-5 Pa. $4.00

LONDON: A PILGRIMAGE, Gustave Doré, Blanchard Jerrold. Squalor, riches, misery, beauty of mid-Victorian metropolis; 55 wonderful plates, 125 other illustrations, full social, cultural text by Jerrold. 191pp. of text. 8⅛ x 11.
22306-X Pa. $6.00

THE COMPLETE WOODCUTS OF ALBRECHT DÜRER, edited by Dr. W. Kurth. 346 in all: Old Testament, St. Jerome, Passion, Life of Virgin, Apocalypse, many others. Introduction by Campbell Dodgson. 285pp. 8½ x 12¼.   21097-9 Pa. $6.00

THE DISASTERS OF WAR, Francisco Goya. 83 etchings record horrors of Napoleonic wars in Spain and war in general. Reprint of 1st edition, plus 3 additional plates. Introduction by Philip Hofer. 97pp. 9⅜ x 8¼.   21872-4 Pa. $3.50

ENGRAVINGS OF HOGARTH, William Hogarth. 101 of Hogarth's greatest works: Rake's Progress, Harlot's Progress, Illustrations for Hudibras, Midnight Modern Conversation, Before and After, Beer Street and Gin Lane, many more. Full commentary. 256pp. 11 x 14.   22479-1 Pa. $7.95

PRIMITIVE ART, Franz Boas. Great anthropologist on ceramics, textiles, wood, stone, metal, etc.; patterns, technology, symbols, styles. All areas, but fullest on Northwest Coast Indians. 350 illustrations. 378pp.   20025-6 Pa. $3.75

MOTHER GOOSE'S MELODIES. Facsimile of fabulously rare Munroe and Francis "copyright 1833" Boston edition. Familiar and unusual rhymes, wonderful old woodcut illustrations. Edited by E.F. Bleiler. 128pp. 4½ x 6⅜. 22577-1 Pa. $1.50

MOTHER GOOSE IN HIEROGLYPHICS. Favorite nursery rhymes presented in rebus form for children. Fascinating 1849 edition reproduced in toto, with key. Introduction by E.F. Bleiler. About 400 woodcuts. 64pp. 6⅞ x 5¼. 20745-5 Pa. $1.50

PETER PIPER'S PRACTICAL PRINCIPLES OF PLAIN & PERFECT PRONUNCIATION. Alliterative jingles and tongue-twisters. Reproduction in full of 1830 first American edition. 25 spirited woodcuts. 32pp. 4½ x 6⅜. 22560-7 Pa. $1.25

MARMADUKE MULTIPLY'S MERRY METHOD OF MAKING MINOR MATHEMATICIANS. Fellow to Peter Piper, it teaches multiplication table by catchy rhymes and woodcuts. 1841 Munroe & Francis edition. Edited by E.F. Bleiler. 103pp. 4⅝ x 6. 22773-1 Pa. $1.25

THE NIGHT BEFORE CHRISTMAS, Clement Moore. Full text, and woodcuts from original 1848 book. Also critical, historical material. 19 illustrations. 40pp. 4⅝ x 6. 22797-9 Pa. $1.35

THE KING OF THE GOLDEN RIVER, John Ruskin. Victorian children's classic of three brothers, their attempts to reach the Golden River, what becomes of them. Facsimile of original 1889 edition. 22 illustrations. 56pp. 4⅝ x 6⅜. 20066-3 Pa. $1.50

DREAMS OF THE RAREBIT FIEND, Winsor McCay. Pioneer cartoon strip, unexcelled for beauty, imagination, in 60 full sequences. Incredible technical virtuosity, wonderful visual wit. Historical introduction. 62pp. 8⅜ x 11¼. 21347-1 Pa. $2.50

THE KATZENJAMMER KIDS, Rudolf Dirks. In full color, 14 strips from 1906-7; full of imagination, characteristic humor. Classic of great historical importance. Introduction by August Derleth. 32pp. 9¼ x 12¼. 23005-8 Pa. $2.00

LITTLE ORPHAN ANNIE AND LITTLE ORPHAN ANNIE IN COSMIC CITY, Harold Gray. Two great sequences from the early strips: our curly-haired heroine defends the Warbucks' financial empire and, then, takes on meanie Phineas P. Pinchpenny. Leapin' lizards! 178pp. 6⅛ x 8⅜. 23107-0 Pa. $2.00

ABSOLUTELY MAD INVENTIONS, A.E. Brown, H.A. Jeffcott. Hilarious, useless, or merely absurd inventions all granted patents by the U.S. Patent Office. Edible tie pin, mechanical hat tipper, etc. 57 illustrations. 125pp. 22596-8 Pa. $1.50

THE DEVIL'S DICTIONARY, Ambrose Bierce. Barbed, bitter, brilliant witticisms in the form of a dictionary. Best, most ferocious satire America has produced. 145pp. 20487-1 Pa. $1.75

THE BEST DR. THORNDYKE DETECTIVE STORIES, R. Austin Freeman. The Case of Oscar Brodski, The Moabite Cipher, and 5 other favorites featuring the great scientific detective, plus his long-believed-lost first adventure — 31 New Inn — reprinted here for the first time. Edited by E.F. Bleiler. USO 20388-3 Pa. $3.00

BEST "THINKING MACHINE" DETECTIVE STORIES, Jacques Futrelle. The Problem of Cell 13 and 11 other stories about Prof. Augustus S.F.X. Van Dusen, including two "lost" stories. First reprinting of several. Edited by E.F. Bleiler. 241pp.
20537-1 Pa. $3.00

UNCLE SILAS, J. Sheridan LeFanu. Victorian Gothic mystery novel, considered by many best of period, even better than Collins or Dickens. Wonderful psychological terror. Introduction by Frederick Shroyer. 436pp.   21715-9 Pa. $4.50

BEST DR. POGGIOLI DETECTIVE STORIES, T.S. Stribling. 15 best stories from EQMM and The Saint offer new adventures in Mexico, Florida, Tennessee hills as Poggioli unravels mysteries and combats Count Jalacki. 217pp.   23227-1 Pa. $3.00

EIGHT DIME NOVELS, selected with an introduction by E.F. Bleiler. Adventures of Old King Brady, Frank James, Nick Carter, Deadwood Dick, Buffalo Bill, The Steam Man, Frank Merriwell, and Horatio Alger — 1877 to 1905. Important, entertaining popular literature in facsimile reprint, with original covers. 190pp. 9 x 12.   22975-0 Pa. $3.50

ALICE'S ADVENTURES UNDER GROUND, Lewis Carroll. Facsimile of ms. Carroll gave Alice Liddell in 1864. Different in many ways from final Alice. Handlettered, illustrated by Carroll. Introduction by Martin Gardner. 128pp. 21482-6 Pa. $2.00

ALICE IN WONDERLAND COLORING BOOK, Lewis Carroll. Pictures by John Tenniel. Large-size versions of the famous illustrations of Alice, Cheshire Cat, Mad Hatter and all the others, waiting for your crayons. Abridged text. 36 illustrations. 64pp. 8¼ x 11.   22853-3 Pa. $1.50

AVENTURES D'ALICE AU PAYS DES MERVEILLES, Lewis Carroll. Bué's translation of "Alice" into French, supervised by Carroll himself. Novel way to learn language. (No English text.) 42 Tenniel illustrations. 196pp.   22836-3 Pa. $3.00

MYTHS AND FOLK TALES OF IRELAND, Jeremiah Curtin. 11 stories that are Irish versions of European fairy tales and 9 stories from the Fenian cycle — 20 tales of legend and magic that comprise an essential work in the history of folklore. 256pp.   22430-9 Pa. $3.00

EAST O' THE SUN AND WEST O' THE MOON, George W. Dasent. Only full edition of favorite, wonderful Norwegian fairytales — Why the Sea is Salt, Boots and the Troll, etc. — with 77 illustrations by Kittelsen & Werenskiöld. 418pp.
22521-6 Pa. $4.50

PERRAULT'S FAIRY TALES, Charles Perrault and Gustave Doré. Original versions of Cinderella, Sleeping Beauty, Little Red Riding Hood, etc. in best translation, with 34 wonderful illustrations by Gustave Doré. 117pp. 8⅛ x 11.   22311-6 Pa. $2.50

EARLY NEW ENGLAND GRAVESTONE RUBBINGS, Edmund V. Gillon, Jr. 43 photographs, 226 rubbings show heavily symbolic, macabre, sometimes humorous primitive American art. Up to early 19th century. 207pp. 8⅜ x 11¼.
21380-3 Pa. $4.00

L.J.M. DAGUERRE: THE HISTORY OF THE DIORAMA AND THE DAGUERREOTYPE, Helmut and Alison Gernsheim. Definitive account. Early history, life and work of Daguerre; discovery of daguerreotype process; diffusion abroad; other early photography. 124 illustrations. 226pp. 6⅙ x 9¼.
22290-X Pa. $4.00

PHOTOGRAPHY AND THE AMERICAN SCENE, Robert Taft. The basic book on American photography as art, recording form, 1839-1889. Development, influence on society, great photographers, types (portraits, war, frontier, etc.), whatever else needed. Inexhaustible. Illustrated with 322 early photos, daguerreotypes, tintypes, stereo slides, etc. 546pp. 6⅛ x 9¼.
21201-7 Pa. $6.00

PHOTOGRAPHIC SKETCHBOOK OF THE CIVIL WAR, Alexander Gardner. Reproduction of 1866 volume with 100 on-the-field photographs: Manassas, Lincoln on battlefield, slave pens, etc. Introduction by E.F. Bleiler. 224pp. 10¾ x 9.
22731-6 Pa. $6.00

THE MOVIES: A PICTURE QUIZ BOOK, Stanley Appelbaum & Hayward Cirker. Match stars with their movies, name actors and actresses, test your movie skill with 241 stills from 236 great movies, 1902-1959. Indexes of performers and films. 128pp. 8⅜ x 9¼.
20222-4 Pa. $3.00

THE TALKIES, Richard Griffith. Anthology of features, articles from Photoplay, 1928-1940, reproduced complete. Stars, famous movies, technical features, fabulous ads, etc.; Garbo, Chaplin, King Kong, Lubitsch, etc. 4 color plates, scores of illustrations. 327pp. 8⅜ x 11¼.
22762-6 Pa. $6.95

THE MOVIE MUSICAL FROM VITAPHONE TO "42ND STREET," edited by Miles Kreuger. Relive the rise of the movie musical as reported in the pages of Photoplay magazine (1926-1933): every movie review, cast list, ad, and record review; every significant feature article, production still, biography, forecast, and gossip story. Profusely illustrated. 367pp. 8⅜ x 11¼.
23154-2 Pa. $7.95

JOHANN SEBASTIAN BACH, Philipp Spitta. Great classic of biography, musical commentary, with hundreds of pieces analyzed. Also good for Bach's contemporaries. 450 musical examples. Total of 1799pp.
EUK 22278-0, 22279-9 Clothbd., Two vol. set $25.00

BEETHOVEN AND HIS NINE SYMPHONIES, Sir George Grove. Thorough history, analysis, commentary on symphonies and some related pieces. For either beginner or advanced student. 436 musical passages. 407pp.
20334-4 Pa. $4.00

MOZART AND HIS PIANO CONCERTOS, Cuthbert Girdlestone. The only full-length study. Detailed analyses of all 21 concertos, sources; 417 musical examples. 509pp.
21271-8 Pa. $6.00

THE FITZWILLIAM VIRGINAL BOOK, edited by J. Fuller Maitland, W.B. Squire. Famous early 17th century collection of keyboard music, 300 works by Morley, Byrd, Bull, Gibbons, etc. Modern notation. Total of 938pp. 8⅜ x 11.
ECE 21068-5, 21069-3 Pa., Two vol. set $15.00

COMPLETE STRING QUARTETS, Wolfgang A. Mozart. Breitkopf and Härtel edition. All 23 string quartets plus alternate slow movement to K156. Study score. 277pp. 9⅜ x 12¼.
22372-8 Pa. $6.00

COMPLETE SONG CYCLES, Franz Schubert. Complete piano, vocal music of Die Schöne Müllerin, Die Winterreise, Schwanengesang. Also Drinker English singing translations. Breitkopf and Härtel edition. 217pp. 9⅜ x 12¼.
22649-2 Pa. $5.00

THE COMPLETE PRELUDES AND ETUDES FOR PIANOFORTE SOLO, Alexander Scriabin. All the preludes and etudes including many perfectly spun miniatures. Edited by K.N. Igumnov and Y.I. Mil'shteyn. 250pp. 9 x 12.
22919-X Pa. $6.00

TRISTAN UND ISOLDE, Richard Wagner. Full orchestral score with complete instrumentation. Do not confuse with piano reduction. Commentary by Felix Mottl, great Wagnerian conductor and scholar. Study score. 655pp. 8⅛ x 11.
22915-7 Pa. $11.95

FAVORITE SONGS OF THE NINETIES, ed. Robert Fremont. Full reproduction, including covers, of 88 favorites: Ta-Ra-Ra-Boom-De-Aye, The Band Played On, Bird in a Gilded Cage, Under the Bamboo Tree, After the Ball, etc. 401pp. 9 x 12.
EBE 21536-9 Pa. $6.95

SOUSA'S GREAT MARCHES IN PIANO TRANSCRIPTION: ORIGINAL SHEET MUSIC OF 23 WORKS, John Philip Sousa. Selected by Lester S. Levy. Playing edition includes: The Stars and Stripes Forever, The Thunderer, The Gladiator, King Cotton, Washington Post, much more. 24 illustrations. 111pp. 9 x 12.
USO 23132-1 Pa. $3.50

CLASSIC PIANO RAGS, selected with an introduction by Rudi Blesh. Best ragtime music (1897-1922) by Scott Joplin, James Scott, Joseph F. Lamb, Tom Turpin, 9 others. Printed from best original sheet music, plus covers. 364pp. 9 x 12.
EBE 20469-3 Pa. $7.50

ANALYSIS OF CHINESE CHARACTERS, C.D. Wilder, J.H. Ingram. 1000 most important characters analyzed according to primitives, phonetics, historical development. Traditional method offers mnemonic aid to beginner, intermediate student of Chinese, Japanese. 365pp.
23045-7 Pa. $4.00

MODERN CHINESE: A BASIC COURSE, Faculty of Peking University. Self study, classroom course in modern Mandarin. Records contain phonetics, vocabulary, sentences, lessons. 249 page book contains all recorded text, translations, grammar, vocabulary, exercises. Best course on market. 3 12" 33⅓ monaural records, book, album.
98832-5 Set $12.50

MANUAL OF THE TREES OF NORTH AMERICA, Charles S. Sargent. The basic survey of every native tree and tree-like shrub, 717 species in all. Extremely full descriptions, information on habitat, growth, locales, economics, etc. Necessary to every serious tree lover. Over 100 finding keys. 783 illustrations. Total of 986pp.
20277-1, 20278-X Pa., Two vol. set $9.00

BIRDS OF THE NEW YORK AREA, John Bull. Indispensable guide to more than 400 species within a hundred-mile radius of Manhattan. Information on range, status, breeding, migration, distribution trends, etc. Foreword by Roger Tory Peterson. 17 drawings; maps. 540pp.
23222-0 Pa. $6.00

THE SEA-BEACH AT EBB-TIDE, Augusta Foote Arnold. Identify hundreds of marine plants and animals: algae, seaweeds, squids, crabs, corals, etc. Descriptions cover food, life cycle, size, shape, habitat. Over 600 drawings. 490pp.
21949-6 Pa.$5.00

THE MOTH BOOK, William J. Holland. Identify more than 2,000 moths of North America. General information, precise species descriptions. 623 illustrations plus 48 color plates show almost all species, full size. 1968 edition. Still the basic book. Total of 551pp. 6½ x 9¼.
21948-8 Pa. $6.00

HOW INDIANS USE WILD PLANTS FOR FOOD, MEDICINE & CRAFTS, Frances Densmore. Smithsonian, Bureau of American Ethnology report presents wealth of material on nearly 200 plants used by Chippewas of Minnesota and Wisconsin. 33 plates plus 122pp. of text. 6⅛ x 9¼.
23019-8 Pa. $2.50

OLD NEW YORK IN EARLY PHOTOGRAPHS, edited by Mary Black. Your only chance to see New York City as it was 1853-1906, through 196 wonderful photographs from N.Y. Historical Society. Great Blizzard, Lincoln's funeral procession, great buildings. 228pp. 9 x 12.
22907-6 Pa. $6.95

THE AMERICAN REVOLUTION, A PICTURE SOURCEBOOK, John Grafton. Wonderful Bicentennial picture source, with 411 illustrations (contemporary and 19th century) showing battles, personalities, maps, events, flags, posters, soldier's life, ships, etc. all captioned and explained. A wonderful browsing book, supplement to other historical reading. 160pp. 9 x 12.
23226-3 Pa. $4.00

PERSONAL NARRATIVE OF A PILGRIMAGE TO AL-MADINAH AND MECCAH, Richard Burton. Great travel classic by remarkably colorful personality. Burton, disguised as a Moroccan, visited sacred shrines of Islam, narrowly escaping death. Wonderful observations of Islamic life, customs, personalities. 47 illustrations. Total of 959pp.
21217-3, 21218-1 Pa., Two vol. set$10.00

INCIDENTS OF TRAVEL IN CENTRAL AMERICA, CHIAPAS, AND YUCATAN, John L. Stephens. Almost single-handed discovery of Maya culture; exploration of ruined cities, monuments, temples; customs of Indians. 115 drawings. 892pp.
22404-X, 22405-8 Pa., Two vol. set $9.00

CONSTRUCTION OF AMERICAN FURNITURE TREASURES, Lester Margon. 344 detail drawings, complete text on constructing exact reproductions of 38 early American masterpieces: Hepplewhite sideboard, Duncan Phyfe drop-leaf table, mantel clock, gate-leg dining table, Pa. German cupboard, more. 38 plates. 54 photographs. 168pp. 8⅜ x 11¼.   23056-2 Pa. $4.00

JEWELRY MAKING AND DESIGN, Augustus F. Rose, Antonio Cirino. Professional secrets revealed in thorough, practical guide: tools, materials, processes; rings, brooches, chains, cast pieces, enamelling, setting stones, etc. Do not confuse with skimpy introductions: beginner can use, professional can learn from it. Over 200 illustrations. 306pp.   21750-7 Pa. $3.00

METALWORK AND ENAMELLING, Herbert Maryon. Generally conceded best all-around book. Countless trade secrets: materials, tools, soldering, filigree, setting, inlay, niello, repoussé, casting, polishing, etc. For beginner or expert. Author was foremost British expert. 330 illustrations. 335pp.   22702-2 Pa. $4.00

WEAVING WITH FOOT-POWER LOOMS, Edward F. Worst. Setting up a loom, beginning to weave, constructing equipment, using dyes, more, plus over 285 drafts of traditional patterns including Colonial and Swedish weaves. More than 200 other figures. For beginning and advanced. 275pp. 8¾ x 6⅜.   23064-3 Pa. $4.50

WEAVING A NAVAJO BLANKET, Gladys A. Reichard. Foremost anthropologist studied under Navajo women, reveals every step in process from wool, dyeing, spinning, setting up loom, designing, weaving. Much history, symbolism. With this book you could make one yourself. 97 illustrations. 222pp.   22992-0 Pa. $3.00

NATURAL DYES AND HOME DYEING, Rita J. Adrosko. Use natural ingredients: bark, flowers, leaves, lichens, insects etc. Over 135 specific recipes from historical sources for cotton, wool, other fabrics. Genuine premodern handicrafts. 12 illustrations. 160pp.   22688-3 Pa. $2.00

DRIED FLOWERS, Sarah Whitlock and Martha Rankin. Concise, clear, practical guide to dehydration, glycerinizing, pressing plant material, and more. Covers use of silica gel. 12 drawings. Originally titled "New Techniques with Dried Flowers." 32pp.   21802-3 Pa. $1.00

THOMAS NAST: CARTOONS AND ILLUSTRATIONS, with text by Thomas Nast St. Hill. Father of American political cartooning. Cartoons that destroyed Tweed Ring; inflation, free love, church and state; original Republican elephant and Democratic donkey; Santa Claus; more. 117 illustrations. 146pp. 9 x 12.
22983-1 Pa. $4.00
23067-8 Clothbd. $8.50

FREDERIC REMINGTON: 173 DRAWINGS AND ILLUSTRATIONS. Most famous of the Western artists, most responsible for our myths about the American West in its untamed days. Complete reprinting of Drawings of Frederic Remington (1897), plus other selections. 4 additional drawings in color on covers. 140pp. 9 x 12.
20714-5 Pa. $5.00'

How to Solve Chess Problems, Kenneth S. Howard. Practical suggestions on problem solving for very beginners. 58 two-move problems, 46 3-movers, 8 4-movers for practice, plus hints. 171pp. 20748-X Pa. **$3.00**

A Guide to Fairy Chess, Anthony Dickins. 3-D chess, 4-D chess, chess on a cylindrical board, reflecting pieces that bounce off edges, cooperative chess, retrograde chess, maximummers, much more. Most based on work of great Dawson. Full handbook, 100 problems. 66pp. 7⅞ x 10¾. 22687-5 Pa. **$2.00**

Win at Backgammon, Millard Hopper. Best opening moves, running game, blocking game, back game, tables of odds, etc. Hopper makes the game clear enough for anyone to play, and win. 43 diagrams. 111pp. 22894-0 Pa. **$1.50**

Bidding a Bridge Hand, Terence Reese. Master player "thinks out loud" the binding of 75 hands that defy point count systems. Organized by bidding problem—no-fit situations, overbidding, underbidding, cueing your defense, etc. 254pp. EBE 22830-4 Pa. **$3.00**

The Precision Bidding System in Bridge, C.C. Wei, edited by Alan Truscott. Inventor of precision bidding presents average hands and hands from actual play, including games from 1969 Bermuda Bowl where system emerged. 114 exercises. 116pp. 21171-1 Pa. **$2.25**

Learn Magic, Henry Hay. 20 simple, easy-to-follow lessons on magic for the new magician: illusions, card tricks, silks, sleights of hand, coin manipulations, escapes, and more —all with a minimum amount of equipment. Final chapter explains the great stage illusions. 92 illustrations. 285pp. 21238-6 Pa. **$2.95**

The New Magician's Manual, Walter B. Gibson. Step-by-step instructions and clear illustrations guide the novice in mastering 36 tricks; much equipment supplied on 16 pages of cut-out materials. 36 additional tricks. 64 illustrations. 159pp. 6⅝ x 10. 23113-5 Pa. **$3.00**

Professional Magic for Amateurs, Walter B. Gibson. 50 easy, effective tricks used by professionals —cards, string, tumblers, handkerchiefs, mental magic, etc. 63 illustrations. 223pp. 23012-0 Pa. **$2.50**

Card Manipulations, Jean Hugard. Very rich collection of manipulations; has taught thousands of fine magicians tricks that are really workable, eye-catching. Easily followed, serious work. Over 200 illustrations. 163pp. 20539-8 Pa. **$2.00**

Abbott's Encyclopedia of Rope Tricks for Magicians, Stewart James. Complete reference book for amateur and professional magicians containing more than 150 tricks involving knots, penetrations, cut and restored rope, etc. 510 illustrations. Reprint of 3rd edition. 400pp. 23206-9 Pa. **$3.50**

The Secrets of Houdini, J.C. Cannell. Classic study of Houdini's incredible magic, exposing closely-kept professional secrets and revealing, in general terms, the whole art of stage magic. 67 illustrations. 279pp. 22913-0 Pa. **$3.00**

THE MAGIC MOVING PICTURE BOOK, Bliss, Sands & Co. The pictures in this book move! Volcanoes erupt, a house burns, a serpentine dancer wiggles her way through a number. By using a specially ruled acetate screen provided, you can obtain these and 15 other startling effects. Originally "The Motograph Moving Picture Book." 32pp. 8¼ x 11.   23224-7 Pa. $1.75

STRING FIGURES AND HOW TO MAKE THEM, Caroline F. Jayne. Fullest, clearest instructions on string figures from around world: Eskimo, Navajo, Lapp, Europe, more. Cats cradle, moving spear, lightning, stars. Introduction by A.C. Haddon. 950 illustrations. 407pp.   20152-X Pa. $3.50

PAPER FOLDING FOR BEGINNERS, William D. Murray and Francis J. Rigney. Clearest book on market for making origami sail boats, roosters, frogs that move legs, cups, bonbon boxes. 40 projects. More than 275 illustrations. Photographs. 94pp.   20713-7 Pa $1.50

INDIAN SIGN LANGUAGE, William Tomkins. Over 525 signs developed by Sioux, Blackfoot, Cheyenne, Arapahoe and other tribes. Written instructions and diagrams: how to make words, construct sentences. Also 290 pictographs of Sioux and Ojibway tribes. 111pp. 6⅛ x 9¼.   22029-X Pa. $1.75

BOOMERANGS: HOW TO MAKE AND THROW THEM, Bernard S. Mason. Easy to make and throw, dozens of designs: cross-stick, pinwheel, boomabird, tumblestick, Australian curved stick boomerang. Complete throwing instructions. All safe. 99pp.   23028-7 Pa. $1.75

25 KITES THAT FLY, Leslie Hunt. Full, easy to follow instructions for kites made from inexpensive materials. Many novelties. Reeling, raising, designing your own. 70 illustrations. 110pp.   22550-X Pa. $1.50

TRICKS AND GAMES ON THE POOL TABLE, Fred Herrmann. 79 tricks and games, some solitaires, some for 2 or more players, some competitive; mystifying shots and throws, unusual carom, tricks involving cork, coins, a hat, more. 77 figures. 95pp.   21814-7 Pa. $1.50

WOODCRAFT AND CAMPING, Bernard S. Mason. How to make a quick emergency shelter, select woods that will burn immediately, make do with limited supplies, etc. Also making many things out of wood, rawhide, bark, at camp. Formerly titled Woodcraft. 295 illustrations. 580pp.   21951-8 Pa. $4.00

AN INTRODUCTION TO CHESS MOVES AND TACTICS SIMPLY EXPLAINED, Leonard Barden. Informal intermediate introduction: reasons for moves, tactics, openings, traps, positional play, endgame. Isolates patterns. 102pp. USO 21210-6 Pa. $1.35

LASKER'S MANUAL OF CHESS, Dr. Emanuel Lasker. Great world champion offers very thorough coverage of all aspects of chess. Combinations, position play, openings, endgame, aesthetics of chess, philosophy of struggle, much more. Filled with analyzed games. 390pp.   20640-8 Pa. $4.00

SLEEPING BEAUTY, illustrated by Arthur Rackham. Perhaps the fullest, most delightful version ever, told by C.S. Evans. Rackham's best work. 49 illustrations. 110pp. 7⅞ x 10¾. 22756-1 Pa. $2.00

THE WONDERFUL WIZARD OF OZ, L. Frank Baum. Facsimile in full color of America's finest children's classic. Introduction by Martin Gardner. 143 illustrations by W.W. Denslow. 267pp. 20691-2 $3.50

GOOPS AND HOW TO BE THEM, Gelett Burgess. Classic tongue-in-cheek masquerading as etiquette book. 87 verses, 170 cartoons as Goops demonstrate virtues of table manners, neatness, courtesy, more. 88pp. 6½ x 9¼.
22233-0 Pa. $2.00

THE BROWNIES, THEIR BOOK, Palmer Cox. Small as mice, cunning as foxes, exuberant, mischievous, Brownies go to zoo, toy shop, seashore, circus, more. 24 verse adventures. 266 illustrations. 144pp. 6⅝ x 9¼. 21265-3 Pa. $2.50

BILLY WHISKERS: THE AUTOBIOGRAPHY OF A GOAT, Frances Trego Montgomery. Escapades of that rambunctious goat. Favorite from turn of the century America. 24 illustrations. 259pp. 22345-0 Pa. $2.75

THE ROCKET BOOK, Peter Newell. Fritz, janitor's kid, sets off rocket in basement of apartment house; an ingenious hole punched through every page traces course of rocket. 22 duotone drawings, verses. 48pp. 6⅞ x 8⅜. 22044-3 Pa. $1.50

CUT AND COLOR PAPER MASKS, Michael Grater. Clowns, animals, funny faces . . . simply color them in, cut them out, and put them together, and you have 9 paper masks to play with and enjoy. Complete instructions. Assembled masks shown in full color on the covers. 32pp. 8¼ x 11. 23171-2 Pa. $1.50

THE TALE OF PETER RABBIT, Beatrix Potter. The inimitable Peter's terrifying adventure in Mr. McGregor's garden, with all 27 wonderful, full-color Potter illustrations. 55pp. 4¼ x 5½. USO 22827-4 Pa. $1.00

THE TALE OF MRS. TIGGY-WINKLE, Beatrix Potter. Your child will love this story about a very special hedgehog and all 27 wonderful, full-color Potter illustrations. 57pp. 4¼ x 5½. USO 20546-0 Pa. $1.00

THE TALE OF BENJAMIN BUNNY, Beatrix Potter. Peter Rabbit's cousin coaxes him back into Mr. McGregor's garden for a whole new set of adventures. A favorite with children. All 27 full-color illustrations. 59pp. 4¼ x 5½.
USO 21102-9 Pa. $1.00

THE MERRY ADVENTURES OF ROBIN HOOD, Howard Pyle. Facsimile of original (1883) edition, finest modern version of English outlaw's adventures. 23 illustrations by Pyle. 296pp. 6½ x 9¼. 22043-5 Pa. $4.00

TWO LITTLE SAVAGES, Ernest Thompson Seton. Adventures of two boys who lived as Indians; explaining Indian ways, woodlore, pioneer methods. 293 illustrations. 286pp. 20985-7 Pa. $3.50

HOUDINI ON MAGIC, Harold Houdini. Edited by Walter Gibson, Morris N. Young. How he escaped; exposés of fake spiritualists; instructions for eye-catching tricks; other fascinating material by and about greatest magician. 155 illustrations. 280pp. 20384-0 Pa. $2.75

HANDBOOK OF THE NUTRITIONAL CONTENTS OF FOOD, U.S. Dept. of Agriculture. Largest, most detailed source of food nutrition information ever prepared. Two mammoth tables: one measuring nutrients in 100 grams of edible portion; the other, in edible portion of 1 pound as purchased. Originally titled Composition of Foods. 190pp. 9 x 12. 21342-0 Pa. $4.00

COMPLETE GUIDE TO HOME CANNING, PRESERVING AND FREEZING, U.S. Dept. of Agriculture. Seven basic manuals with full instructions for jams and jellies; pickles and relishes; canning fruits, vegetables, meat; freezing anything. Really good recipes, exact instructions for optimal results. Save a fortune in food. 156 illustrations. 214pp. 6⅛ x 9¼. 22911-4 Pa. $2.50

THE BREAD TRAY, Louis P. De Gouy. Nearly every bread the cook could buy or make: bread sticks of Italy, fruit breads of Greece, glazed rolls of Vienna, everything from corn pone to croissants. Over 500 recipes altogether. including buns, rolls, muffins, scones, and more. 463pp. 23000-7 Pa. $4.00

CREATIVE HAMBURGER COOKERY, Louis P. De Gouy. 182 unusual recipes for casseroles, meat loaves and hamburgers that turn inexpensive ground meat into memorable main dishes: Arizona chili burgers, burger tamale pie, burger stew, burger corn loaf, burger wine loaf, and more. 120pp. 23001-5 Pa. $1.75

LONG ISLAND SEAFOOD COOKBOOK, J. George Frederick and Jean Joyce. Probably the best American seafood cookbook. Hundreds of recipes. 40 gourmet sauces, 123 recipes using oysters alone! All varieties of fish and seafood amply represented. 324pp. 22677-8 Pa. $3.50

THE EPICUREAN: A COMPLETE TREATISE OF ANALYTICAL AND PRACTICAL STUDIES IN THE CULINARY ART, Charles Ranhofer. Great modern classic. 3,500 recipes from master chef of Delmonico's, turn-of-the-century America's best restaurant. Also explained, many techniques known only to professional chefs. 775 illustrations. 1183pp. 6⅝ x 10. 22680-8 Clothbd. $22.50

THE AMERICAN WINE COOK BOOK, Ted Hatch. Over 700 recipes: old favorites livened up with wine plus many more: Czech fish soup, quince soup, sauce Perigueux, shrimp shortcake, filets Stroganoff, cordon bleu goulash, jambonneau, wine fruit cake, more. 314pp. 22796-0 Pa. $2.50

DELICIOUS VEGETARIAN COOKING, Ivan Baķer. Close to 500 delicious and varied recipes: soups, main course dishes (pea, bean, lentil, cheese, vegetable, pasta, and egg dishes), savories, stews, whole-wheat breads and cakes, more. 168pp. USO 22834-7 Pa. $2.00

COOKIES FROM MANY LANDS, Josephine Perry. Crullers, oatmeal cookies, chaux au chocolate, English tea cakes, mandel kuchen, Sacher torte, Danish puff pastry, Swedish cookies — a mouth-watering collection of 223 recipes. 157pp.

22832-0 Pa. $2.25

ROSE RECIPES, Eleanour S. Rohde. How to make sauces, jellies, tarts, salads, potpourris, sweet bags, pomanders, perfumes from garden roses; all exact recipes. Century old favorites. 95pp.

22957-2 Pa. $1.75

"OSCAR" OF THE WALDORF'S COOKBOOK, Oscar Tschirky. Famous American chef reveals 3455 recipes that made Waldorf great; cream of French, German, American cooking, in all categories. Full instructions, easy home use. 1896 edition. 907pp. 6⅝ x 9⅜.

20790-0 Clothbd. $15.00

JAMS AND JELLIES, May Byron. Over 500 old-time recipes for delicious jams, jellies, marmalades, preserves, and many other items. Probably the largest jam and jelly book in print. Originally titled May Byron's Jam Book. 276pp.

USO 23130-5 Pa. $3.50

MUSHROOM RECIPES, André L. Simon. 110 recipes for everyday and special cooking. Champignons à la grecque, sole bonne femme, chicken liver croustades, more; 9 basic sauces, 13 ways of cooking mushrooms. 54pp.

USO 20913-X Pa. $1.25

THE BUCKEYE COOKBOOK, Buckeye Publishing Company. Over 1,000 easy-to-follow, traditional recipes from the American Midwest: bread (100 recipes alone), meat, game, jam, candy, cake, ice cream, and many other categories of cooking. 64 illustrations. From 1883 enlarged edition. 416pp.

23218-2 Pa. $4.00

TWENTY-TWO AUTHENTIC BANQUETS FROM INDIA, Robert H. Christie. Complete, easy-to-do recipes for almost 200 authentic Indian dishes assembled in 22 banquets. Arranged by region. Selected from Banquets of the Nations. 192pp.

23200-X Pa. $2.50